Praise for *Parklands*

Poignant, punchy and practical, *Parklands: A School Built on Love* is a hard-nosed take on love as a driver for school improvement – and it is heart-warming and heartbreaking in equal measure.

We can't all be Chris, but we can all learn from the way he works.

Mary Myatt, education writer, speaker and curator at Myatt & Co

What a book! What a school! Having been lucky enough to have tears of joy streaming down my face at hearing the whole school roaring out 'Sweet Caroline' not once, but twice, with the entire crowd swaying and dancing, I can testify that Parklands is a school truly built on love.

You'll find more than love in this book, though. There are fundraising ideas, pedagogy ideas, curriculum ideas, competitions, reindeer and fake snow aplenty – and that's only the half of it. An education book to savour! And, finally, upon reading the postscript about Jason, another great big happy tear dribbled down my face too, because what Parklands did for Jason is what they would do for any member of their community.

A stunning achievement, Mr Dyson. My hat is off to you and your school!

Paul Garvey, educational consultant and author

Not only do the Parklands primary school staff exude a passion for working at the school, but Dyson himself embodies in his leadership how a school can be led with rigour and love, rather than accountability and discipline. Not all schools are led in this way, and sadly not every teacher loves the school they teach in.

Parklands is a stand-out memory for me and I encourage you to visit; this book provides only a glimpse into the miracles that happen there day-to-day, behind the scenes.

Ross McGill, founder of @TeacherToolkit

The Parklands story is an incredible example of the power of great leadership, lots of laughter and (in the very words of the author) big love! For all leaders, and not just those working in education, this book is a must-read if you're interested in creating transformational change.

Drew Povey, leadership specialist and performance coach

I have been in education for 57 years and have worked in so very many wonderful schools with outstanding staff, leadership and ethos, yet I can honestly say – hand on heart – I have never experienced the consistent and absolute belonging and love that envelops every single child in Parklands Primary School. The joy, when within school, of the many impoverished children at Parklands is overwhelming and brings a huge smile to my face and an occasional tear to my eye.

This book celebrates the saving of a school in one of the most deprived districts in the country, after years of crisis and conflict. It tells the story of how the absolute love and commitment of one head teacher won over the hearts and minds of the children, the staff and the families the school serves. It tracks the journey of not only changing the culture of the school but of instilling a huge love of learning and a shared pride in the amazing standards of achievement now seen in all they do.

**Ros Wilson, education consultant, public speaker, blogger,
podcaster, and creator and author of Talk:Write**

Parklands: A School Built on Love captures the energy and empathy that you experience when you visit the school. It offers an insight into the wholehearted and warm-hearted commitment of everyone who works in the school and illuminates how and why every child at Parklands develops a love for learning and achievement. It also highlights what is possible when a school connects with, and responds to, the lived experience and needs of their community. Chris Dyson's love for what he does shines throughout.

**Professor Tim O'Brien, Department of Psychology and
Human Development, UCL Institute of Education**

Having had the privilege of working as SENDCo at Parklands for just over three years before retiring, I am one of the lucky ones to have experienced and contributed to the love that underpins and drives the school.

This book beautifully sums up the force of nature that is Chris Dyson and the full-on journey of the Parklands team to turn the school around with high expectations, consistency, respect, inclusion, team work, music and hearts full of love. There is something for everyone working in schools today to take away and adapt for their own setting.

Beth Bennett, retired teacher, deputy head teacher and SENDCo

Parklands isn't just a school; it does everything it can to be the beating heart of the community, a heart filled with love. Not the saccharine Valentine's card love, but the deep unconditional love you reserve for family. That's because everyone who is in the Parklands Community *is* family.

And Chris Dyson invites everyone in to be part of that family.

Locking your community outside the school gate builds barriers; getting them through wide-open doors and making them feel welcome builds trust, relationships and a sense of belonging. This book shares how Chris and the staff at Parklands have built all of that and used it as a launch pad for the success of their pupils.

Ben Brown, founder of Education Roundtables

This book is an easy read, full of useful tips for aspiring leaders. Chris shares the journey of the Parklands team in turning around a school and its community. A turnaround based on love – and not the fluffy kind, but a 'love that is full of hope, ambition and the highest expectations'.

The book is also brought up to date with a postscript which reduced me to tears then made me howl with laughter.

Highly recommended.

Raj Unsworth, Chair, Greenwood Academies Trust, HR professional,
and advisor to Headteachers' Roundtable

There is an honesty, a passion and an integrity that shines throughout this book, sprinkled with snippets of humour – and these combine to make for a fascinating and engaging read. It provides an in-depth insight into what makes Parklands such an exceptional school for children, staff, parents and governors; teamwork, the enrichment of experiences, and the securing and allocation of resources are notable features. A visit to this school totally validates the book's key messages – the sharing in an atmosphere of engagement and challenge, of innovation and variety, of care and warmth – a school that serves, supports and challenges its community in equal measure, where love and safeguarding go hand in hand, where children are happy, flourish and excel.

This is the sort of school I wish I had attended as a child when growing up in what was euphemistically described as 'an education priority area'. If only the Parklands' priorities described in this book had been similarly identified and addressed then! Parklands is a school that every child deserves.

To every teacher, to every aspiring leader (whatever area you work in), read this book – and, if possible, visit the school. You will not be disappointed!

John Sharpe, consultant school improvement adviser,
TES author and former head teacher

Parklands
A school built on love

Chris Dyson

Crown House Publishing Limited
www.crownhouse.co.uk

Published by
Crown House Publishing
Crown Buildings, Bancyfelin, Carmarthen, Wales, SA33 5ND, UK
www.crownhouse.co.uk

and

Crown House Publishing Company LLC
PO Box 2223, Williston, VT 05495, USA
www.crownhousepublishing.com

British Library of Cataloguing-in-Publication Data
A catalogue entry for this book is available from the British Library.

Print ISBN 978-178583600-8
Mobi ISBN 978-178583620-6
ePub ISBN 978-178583621-3
ePDF ISBN 978-178583622-0

LCCN 2021950839

Printed and bound in the UK by
TJ Books, Padstow, Cornwall

Foreword

"Ere, mister … You them visitors what have come't see school?"

The small moon-faced boy beamed up at us. He had been waiting for our arrival and pounced on us the very moment we set foot in the door.

It had taken four-and-a-half hours to travel from Bristol to Leeds through ever gloomier weather. We arrived at Parklands Primary, swathed in grey drizzle, on a particularly grim Thursday afternoon. I had warned my colleagues from South Gloucestershire that the North would indeed be grim, and on first impressions it didn't disappoint.

'Do you think we've come to the right place?' commented one of my delegation as we picked our way through a desolate car park towards the worn-looking building beyond. We had heard great things about Parklands, but this school was no gleaming temple to modern architecture – quite the opposite. Outwardly, it was a tired-looking place and was surrounded by a similarly tired-looking housing estate. Yet, it was famed for outstanding learning (both in terms of Ofsted judgement, stratospheric outcomes and national reputation).

What we found inside Parklands Primary wasn't outstanding. It was a kind of magic. The success of Parklands Primary School is mind-boggling!

Judged outstanding in September 2017, its outcomes are eye-watering (especially in maths where it scored a progress measure of +5.2 in 2018 and +8.5 in 2017, and last year had 75% of children achieve greater depth). It also serves one of the most deprived estates in Yorkshire with 72% of children in receipt of the pupil premium. That is right, 72% of children are pupil premium; 75% of children achieved greater depth in maths in 2018.

I have thought long and hard about how to describe the relationships which underpin everything that happens at Parklands. It does not feel like any school I have ever visited. And love is the only word that fits. Seconds after the moon-faced boy had welcomed us, Chris Dyson, the irrepressible head teacher, dashes past. 'Stewy!' he bellows, not in anger but in sheer delight. The moon-faced boy (Stewy – as I learned the head teacher had nicknamed him) beamed from ear to ear and the two of them exchanged an in-joke. The staff at Parklands love the children like their own.

I later discovered that Stewy, our guide for the day, had been permanently excluded from two other schools. Yet, here he was, happy, relaxed and extremely polite. Trusted to show six head teachers around his school. It was the same in every interaction with every member of staff. Behaviour was exceptional in every room we visited (and we were allowed to roam at will, without a member of staff to guide us away from any class of unruly pupils which could embarrass the school's image). The excellent behaviour we saw was offered freely by every child. This was because they knew that every adult they met would care for them as if they were a member of their own family. This was quite confronting.

Parklands, while it too has the usual rules and expectations, also has a deep care for the children which goes above and beyond what you would usually expect to see in even the most exceptional school. Every interaction between adult and child implies that the adults care deeply for the children, and would therefore move heaven and earth in order to ensure they succeed.

The pupils at Parklands often face significant hardship. Much of the housing on the estate is poor and overcrowded; poverty is grinding, bringing with it all the social ills that this creates. The children start at the school significantly behind their peers nationally, especially with their speech and language.

It would be very tempting to throw your hands in the air and conclude that, whatever the school does, nothing can counter this tsunami of dis-advantage. It would be easy to talk about this barrier or that barrier as a way of (reasonably) justifying outcomes that are lower than those in more affluent areas. Throughout our visit barriers were never discussed. Indeed, it was as though the staff simply didn't believe in them. This is not to say that the staff aren't aware of the poverty and hardship that most pupils experience – they are extremely aware of it. However, to them, it is a problem that simply must be overcome.

The school employs safeguarding officers whose daily job is to keep the children safe from harm – an indication of the hardship they face. The school has high adult-to-pupil ratios, allowing children the adult time they need to make secure attachments and to learn well.

The school pays for every child from Year 4–6 to take part in an annual residential school camp, providing them with experiences that would otherwise be beyond reach. Likewise, the school's ambitious extracurricular programme provides a wealth of character-affirming opportunities. The school even opens on Christmas Eve. How does it afford this? Chris and his team raise a lot of money!

In 2021, the Parklands staff raised a staggering £500,000 for the school. To say that Chris' approach to fundraising is tenacious is an understatement. Chris is a master salesman (possibly a used-car salesman in a former life), and uses this skill to squeeze money out of the great and the good. His strategy is simple: invite CEOs of large companies to visit his school (never via a generic mailshot, always via a personal email or phone call); show them the abject poverty in which his children live; ask them to help. And help they do – often with donations running into the tens of thousands.

A key focus for my visit to Parklands was to discover the secret to their exceptional outcomes. The answer appears to be found in the school's focus on deliberate, regular practice. Again, it sounds ludicrously simple – keep practising something until it sticks – but, from leading pupil premium reviews myself, it appears that practice is something that many schools have largely overlooked in the clamour for mastery.

The vast majority of children know all their times tables facts by the end of Year 2. Again, no exceptions or excuses are made for vulnerable children – they are expected to learn their tables at exactly the same rate as their peers. The daily timetable is geared towards ensuring that children have the opportunity to master these basic skills through structured practice.

Chris is fiercely proud of Parklands and everything they have achieved, and his drive to ensure that every child succeeds is evident in every leadership decision. He even moved his own children to the school – a very powerful message to the whole school community of the confidence he has in 'the Parklands way'.

He and his staff think very carefully about how to improve teaching and learning. Staff never attend generic courses, but instead read widely about the latest practice. Chris invites high-profile authors to lead bespoke training with staff and then spends significant amounts of time embedding new learning.

Above all, Parklands is one of the happiest schools I have visited. And, again, this is a deliberate strategy to foster the values that the school is seeking to promote – namely, a belief that every child is worthy and capable of success.

All day, every day, positive pop music booms out of the hall's public address system (Parklands is not a quiet place!), and this positivism is infectious to children and visitors alike.

The school's drama productions, along with the many other extracurricular activities, are highly valued by the school community.

Every Friday is called 'Funday Friday' – a day of celebration for all that the school has achieved during the week. Done badly this could just become an empty gimmick, but because it is the physical manifestation of everything the school is about, it is a way of the staff telling every child that they are special.

So, back to the moon-faced boy. "Ere, Stewy,' boomed Chris, 'don't forget your tea!' Throughout our visit an M&S roast beef and Yorkshire pudding meal for one had sat on the head teacher's table. Chris had explained that it was Stewy's favourite and he had bought it for him to say thank you for showing us around. 'It'll be toast for tea otherwise,' he explained.

Stewy collected his beef and Yorkshire pudding meal for one and headed to the door with a broad grin on his face. Then he stopped and looked a bit sheepish. Then he turned around and dashed back towards Chris and gave him an enormous hug. Then (remembering he was a 9-year-old boy who was too cool to hug his head teacher) he made his escape.

So ask yourself this: do you know the favourite dinner of the most vulnerable children in your school? If, like me, you can't answer that question, then maybe, just maybe, we should all aim to be a little bit more like the staff at Parklands Primary School.

Simon Botten[1]

---

1   Adapted from Simon Botten, Do You Believe in Magic? Trip to the North Part 1 – Parklands Primary, Leeds, *SouthGlosHead* [blog] (4 January 2019). Available at: https://southgloshead. wordpress.com/2019/01/04/do-you-believe-in-magic-trip-to-the-north-part-1-parklands-primary-leeds.

Acknowledgements

Make no bones about it: to make a success of a journey you need a team that shares the same ethos, the same drive and the same goals. I have been blessed to work with some amazing teachers, teaching assistants, learning mentors, office staff, cleaners and lunchtime staff. I have been blessed to see my middle leaders grow into senior leaders who drive forward the vision.

Laura, Julia, Katie, Sam, Brooke, Grace, Lucy, Kath and Beth – you made this book possible by taking the greatest set of staff on a journey on the road to excellence.

I am involved in some wonderful WhatsApp groups. All of them offer love, support, giggles and an ear when the stress of the job means you need to sound off.

My very first group was aptly named #TheNicestGangOnTwitter. These wonderful people were present when my bundle of joy, Delphi, was born, and they were there to celebrate my 200th follower on Twitter. Meeting up with them in real life is inspirational.

#113 group was initially football talk, but as we got to know one another more, the group supported and shared ideas more. Well-being is at our core. It was this anonymous group that celebrated the unsung heroes on Twitter by giving them the #GoldenHeart award. Well, that is one secret out of the bag!

#BritainsKindestLeaders has been going for 18 months now. The group was the brainchild of Ben Brown (@EdRoundtables). The COVID-19 pandemic and the problems of the last 18 months were shared among us. The documents shared saved hours of time. The support given on the dark days, as well as the laughter, makes this currently my most used direct message group. The weekend in the Lakes was one of the best well-being experiences ever.

Jean Hirst, our school improvement adviser, and my wonderful governors challenge when they need to challenge and support when they need to support. Straight-talking and no waffle makes sure the school is on a path to excellence. Jean was my mentor and moulded me into the leader I am today. Without Jean, Parklands would not be Parklands.

Ian Stokes (@IanStokesEd) is the data man who joined the dots and showcased the school's data. I met Ian and played cricket with him for 13 years as part of Education Leeds when I was a deputy head teacher. He watched me grow from a deputy to a head. His data work celebrated the successes and, more importantly, identified where the next improvements were needed. This helped to form the school improvement plan. His work was direct and to the point, and made the data discussions with Ofsted go with ease. A true friend and a true part of the Parklands DNA.

Adam Smith (@MrJunkFoodChef) and I teamed up in my first year at Parklands, and the impact he has had has been immense. Adam wants food in tummies, not in bins. His mission was to ensure that no child went hungry. Adam and the Real Junk Food team ensured we had a free market stall two days a week, meaning that everyone who wanted food had it. We do this 52 weeks a year because food hunger doesn't disappear in the holidays. Adam made 22 May 2020 (my daughter's birthday) the happiest day of my teaching career. We distributed 35,000 meals in three hours to ensure that nobody went hungry during lockdown. Parklands and I owe a great deal to Adam.

Mike Harvey (@mikeharvey303) from Business in the Community has been a huge part of the Parklands story. We are blessed with the money that we bring into Parklands. Mike was the inspiration behind this; no Mike Harvey and the journey would have been very different. I had worked with Mike as a deputy head teacher, so I was delighted when we met up again at Parklands in my first term as head teacher (see Chapter 8).

Ruth Lions was a huge influence on my career. At Five Lanes Primary School she made me Key Stage 2 leader. She was the one who taught me that age doesn't matter. If you are good enough or effective enough, you can motivate people and you can lead. It was the first time I had seen a true meritocracy, where the age of the leader didn't reflect their position in the hierarchy. Progression wasn't based on age, it was based on skill. And I had ambition.

It is important to mention Laura Darley – my deputy, my colleague, my friend and my inspiration. I feel emotional writing this because without Laura, the journey would not have been so much fun. Laura started at Parklands as a supply teacher, but her skill in the classroom soon saw her offered a permanent position. When I joined, she was acting assistant head teacher. I remember, prior to beginning work, having a meeting with Laura and the deputy head teacher, Kath Hartley. I said, 'September is the start of something new and something special.' I promised them that we would do it together; there would be highs and lows, but if we stuck together we would succeed. We were doing this as a team.

When Kath relocated to Australia, I had the chance to bring in a new deputy head from outside Parklands, but I had the perfect replacement in Laura. I was a man of my word, and Laura deserved the reward for her dedication to Parklands in her assistant head teacher role. She has grown and grown year on year. She played a huge role in the Ofsted visit and she will one day be the perfect successor to the Parklands headship. An outstanding teacher, leader and friend.

Thanks to Simon Kidwell, Ros Wilson and Beth Bennett for their help and contributions to the book.

Contents

Foreword .... *i*

Acknowledgements .... *vii*

Introduction 1

Chapter 1 Love **5**

Relationships Break Cycles 12

Safeguarding is Love 14

Pastoral and Welfare Teams 18

Parklands Fundamentals 19

Chapter 2 Leadership **21**

Inclusive Leadership, Leading Inclusion 27

Behaviour 29

Leading By Being There 35

Parklands Fundamentals 36

Chapter 3 Learning **37**

Mosque and Crisps 44

SATs and National Testing 46

Parklands SEND 48

Parklands Pedagogy 50

Literally Flying 52

Parklands Fundamentals 53

Chapter 4 Fun Day Friday and the Best Seats in the House **55**

Fun Day Friday 57

Best Seats in the House Assembly 61

Parklands Fundamentals 69

Chapter 5   Looking After Your Staff **71**

Building a New Team from a Broken One 77

Professional Development 78

Last Christmas 82

Parklands Fundamentals 83

Chapter 6   Achievement **85**

Inspection Isn't Always a Dirty Word 89

Early Bird Maths and Same-Day Interventions 92

TES Schools Awards 97

Parklands Fundamentals 98

Chapter 7   Parents, Community and Family **99**

Feeding and Well-being 103

Bringing Food to the Table 104

The Night Before Christmas 106

The Christmas Extravaganza 108

Parklands Fundamentals 115

Chapter 8   Taking Care of Business **117**

Buildings and Maintenance 120

Safeguarding for Visitors 123

Lockdown Laptops 124

Funding 126

Exclusion 128

Parklands Fundamentals 131

Conclusion 133

Postscript: Jason *135*

About the Author *139*

Introduction

Parklands Primary School is on the Seacroft estate in Leeds. It is a larger than average-sized school, and it has 55% of pupils who are eligible for support through the pupil premium, which is more than twice the national average. In 2015, 85% were eligible. The proportion of pupils who have special needs and/or disabilities is well above average. Half of all boys in the school are receiving additional support for special educational needs and/or disabilities. The school has a 21-place resource provision for pupils with severe learning difficulties. Their attainment and progress are included in the overall outcomes for the school. Finally, mobility is above average, so up to a third of pupils join or leave the school during Key Stage 1.

If you were going to prove that there was another way of doing things, there would be easier places to start. But I have never been a fan of the easy path.

When I took over as head teacher there had already been five head teachers in the previous year (myself included). The school was using restraint, isolation booths, a padded cell, heavy sanctions and exclusions in a desperate attempt to wrestle control over behaviour. The community and school were at odds. The curriculum was limited and trust was hard to find. Parklands looked like it could be in a perpetual struggle to raise achievement.

The school needed me and, as we will discover, I needed the school. The stars aligned when I was made head teacher of Parklands, but the dream would take time and hard work to achieve. From being let down and left holding the doughnuts to putting a stop to 'tig on the roof', it has never been easy travelling. But I have never been travelling alone.

The remarkable story of the Parklands team is one that must be heard. A team that was lost and then found itself is the beating heart of the story.

Those early mentors and teachers who walked alongside me and taught me so much are also celebrated here.

This is not a book just about our story, but one that shows you how to grow your school or classroom with love. Love that supports and challenges. Love that drives achievement. Love that has the clearest boundaries. Love that shows itself every day in every interaction.

I will show you how we brought the community onside, why we give children helicopter rides and how music works to drive connection. We will look at building relationships with food, using what you have got to get families what they need and collaborating with business to fully resource your school. I will walk you through Christmas at Parklands and show you the remarkable effect of positive competition in driving achievement.

There is so much more to Parklands. Hidden behind an unassuming 1920s architectural design is a school that is truly remarkable. One that lives the seemingly impossible educational dream of incredibly high achievement, personalised support and complete inclusion.

I hope that you learn something to take into your own setting – that the Parklands experience makes it off the estate and into the national conversation. I hope your school can be a place where there is love but also hope and relentless ambition for our children.

In November 2020, 83% of the school's pupils were living in an area classed as being one of the 10% most deprived areas in England. The Lower Layer Super Output Area (LSOA) in which the school is located is ranked 567th out of 32,844 in terms of deprivation, meaning only 1% of areas in England have higher deprivation. The income, employment, health, education and crime deprivation indicators are all very high. The proportion of people in this area with no qualifications is almost twice as high as the national figure.[1]

Parklands pupil population overview. Data sources: School Information Management System, November 2020; Index of Multiple Deprivation deciles: Ministry of Housing, Communities and Local Government; LSOA boundaries: Office for National Statistics. Contains public sector information licensed under the Open Government Licence v.3.0. Background map images © OpenStreetMap contributors.

1   Ian Stokes Education, *Beyond the School Gates: An Analysis of Demography, Deprivation and Social Context for Parklands Primary School* (Leeds: Ian Stokes Education, 2020), p. 9.

Chapter 1
Love

Chapter 1
Love

When children are at Parklands, when they are in this place, it is like an oasis in the desert. It is totally separate from the Seacroft estate. It is full of smiles, full of hugs and full of music – and these kids respond to that.

At the beating heart of Parklands is love. Unashamed, clear and simple love flows through the culture and daily climate. It drives decision-making throughout the organisation. It is not a love that excuses poor behaviour or lack of achievement. It is not a love that simply wraps children up in emotional warmth (although sometimes that is necessary). It is a love that is full of hope, ambition and the highest expectations. And it is everywhere: in our policies, in our language, in our daily practice, in every conversation with our children or about them.

If you are looking for a strategy, it is love. Start from there. Strip away everything else. Put love in the centre of the page and plan everything from there. Truly. The detail is important. The way we structure learning and teaching has got to be ambitious, drawing in revenue is essential and feeding the community is vital.

At Parklands, love drives it all. We talk about it every day. Everyone does. And if you don't pick it up within 30 seconds of being at Parklands, then you have arrived at the wrong school. It is a whole-team effort – from the teachers and teaching assistants to the office staff, from the lunchtime staff to the governors. With love as a core value, the culture and daily climate is set. People know how to react to difficult situations and how to plan to avoid them. Children trust their teachers, teachers trust their leaders, parents trust their school. Love and trust become like comfy peas in a pod.

But love is not simply an emotion or a lofty value. It is in our strategic thinking as well as our immediate responses. It is present in the big things that Parklands does and in the smallest and the most unremarkable acts. It is demonstrated in our determination to give to our community, and in our belief that their children deserve the very best education. An education as good as any child who is lucky enough to be born with more resources and more structure. Love at Parklands isn't flowery and tear-filled (although we all have our moments). It is practical, not just philosophical. Sometimes it breaks out in sudden and spontaneous moments of beauty. Sometimes it is hidden in anonymous donations or quiet conversations. But, at Parklands, you know you are loved. We quickly give the children the safety and confidence to learn. Our classes are undisrupted. Our school is soaked in positivity.

Everyone at Parklands stops and listens to the children. We are never too busy for them. Ever. Regardless of the perceived importance of a meeting, or the celebrity status of a visitor, or even an intense conversation with a tough inspector, my door is open. Everyone knows I won't turn them away. I have often heard head teachers say, 'My door is always open,' but you still have to make an appointment to see them.

It means that meetings are interrupted by a child who just needs a moment, and phone calls are halted for children who are excited to show me their brilliant work. But we will stop for them. They are always polite – they know to knock – but, at Parklands, the children are too important to be ignored or sidelined. That isn't just a neat statement. It is how we behave in our school.

If the Queen came to visit she would likely experience the same polite but persistent interruptions. We would just pass her the Bourbons (from my private collection) and she could listen to Kara, covered in food dye, telling us about her science practical and sausage breakfast.

You can't tell people that you love them, that they are the most important thing about the school, and then keep your office door closed. Leading by locking yourself away all day isn't going to end well. We have all seen that movie before. Being instantly available means you don't get much peace, but I didn't take the job for a peaceful life. I have never met a visitor who minded being interrupted in a face-to-face meeting or a colleague on a

Zoom call who was fazed by it. At Parklands, the children come first. Everything else can wait a little.

Children and colleagues need you to be present as a head teacher. Not sitting in a comfy chair all day, but walking the floors, going in and out of classrooms, being part of the team. Walking the walk is everything. If you want to be part of the team you need to be visible every day, swimming in the same sea. Spending hours locked in a lifeguard's hut means you might be great in emergencies (as long as someone knocks!), but not in preventing them from happening. Sweep the sheds,[1] stay humble and be available. Sounds simple.

Of course, there is lots of other work to be done, persistently pulling you towards the desk, the computer, the biscuits, the coffee, the peace and quiet. Resist it all. Make your visibility your priority. Every day. The best way to support your colleagues is to stand alongside them. So much time is saved and so many small problems are solved before they become big ones. Your value as a head teacher is not in managing administrative flimflam. Drop some stuff. Delegate it. Find someone else who loves it. Your value lies in being seen, in leading visibly with grace and humility.

I am not a leader because I wanted to escape from the classroom. I became a leader so that I could do more for the children, not less. In practical terms, this means taking work home or delegating tasks that might have been done in school behind a closed door. When you make the children and staff the priority, everything flows from that. A head teacher who professes love and then has an appointment diary, a secretary or a personal assistant is insulated from the real business of culture-building. Culture needs personal attention every day.

---

1   See James Kerr, *Legacy: What the All Blacks Can Teach Us About the Business of Life* (London: Constable & Robinson, 2013). 'Sweeping the sheds' is an example of how everyone needs to be prepared to do any job on behalf of the team.

The Roots of Love

I was born in lovely old Sheffield in 1970 in a suburb called Intake. I had free school meals and free school clothes. In fact, I was the only one in school with free school meals and free school clothes. In the 1970s, fewer married couples got divorced than today. My family was unusual in that my parents did separate, so I felt different. It is one of the reasons that I can relate to the kids at Parklands.

Sadly, I didn't have a dad at home from the age of 8. When he first left home he persisted in wanting to see us for about a year. Then it was just me, my older brother Jonathan and little sister Cherry, and a beautiful mum, grandpa and nan who bestowed us with love. It wasn't about the presents around the Christmas tree, it was about the people around the tree. On occasion, my brother and I went over to our dad's house and played tennis and football all day. The trouble was my brother got to that age when he wanted to see his friends at the weekend more than he wanted to see his dad. I remember my dad phoning up and saying that he either saw all of us or none of us. It broke my heart. We were tough kids but being rejected when I was desperate to see him was harsh. It isn't something I have spoken about before. It still hurts but it also gave me an inner strength, and the love given to us by our mum meant not feeling we had missed out by not having a dad.

I have always loved working in deprived areas because the children show tenacity and never give in. They have got perseverance. They see that you are offering them something – and they take it with both hands. They keep going and going and going. They deserve to be in a place where they belong, where they are important and where they are loved. They deserve to have people around them who love them unconditionally. We are proud to say that Parklands is built on love and stuffed full of compassion.

Relationships Break Cycles

Relationships are two-way at Parklands. We are always happy to be the first to give – and the second, third and so on. We mean that. We don't give up on children and families. We have had way too much success in turning around difficult situations; to try and do it any other way would be madness.

We have learned that there are no quick fixes. We understand that it takes time to build trust. It starts with the school showing they love the children. That is important. Make that the first change you make. When that love is perceived as genuine and heartfelt, then things start to change. Perceived barriers come down, parents open up and everyone focuses on getting the children the best education possible.

It is important to bear in mind that many of the parents who send their children to Parklands haven't had the best experience of education themselves. Don't underestimate the impact of this. We don't just have to get over practical barriers; we are also battling emotional barriers. If your experience of school was to feel failure, that will seep into your children's experience. It affects how you respond to your children's teachers, your attendance at events and parents' evenings, and the conversations about school at home. It can change how you feel about homework, school trips and the attitude you take on behaviour incidents. It might just be the greatest deterrent to a successful education.

There is a cycle that, if it is not challenged, can take a generation of great schooling to break. At Parklands we accelerate it. We work on building trust every day. We show that we love the children and remind them constantly. Conversations that start with love as the foundation are never that difficult.

Money is a persistent hindrance for our parents. We try to take their money worries away, as best we can, when they relate to school. Money can't buy you love, but it can buy you a jumper, a hot dinner, an amazing residential trip, small class sizes and enough adults to make sure you are always supported. If that helps to remove some of the anxiety, then conversations about school are unhindered by financial concerns. It makes school easier for everyone.

If we run schools trips, nobody pays. If there are special events, they are always free. If a family is in need, we will always be there. We are serious about love. We want to have excellent relationships with our community, not just rub along or get by. At Parklands we are never satisfied with that. We need parents along for the ride, properly informed and helped to support their children. If that means making the first move, knocking on the front door and inviting ourselves in for a brew, then that is what we must do. If it means meeting parents on their own terms, then that is what we must do. If it means finding money to allow their children to go further faster, then we will do that too. There are no limits to what people will do when they love someone – or, if there are limits, you won't find them at Parklands.

School cultures are keenly remembered in communities. The reputation of Parklands wasn't always as good as it is now. We have worked hard to turn hearts and minds. Our responsibility as a team of professionals is to stop the cycle of mistrust which builds up in communities when they have had a poor experience of school.

If we want the school to be a beacon of hope, then we have to change that perception and give the children an experience of education that is unerringly positive and life enhancing. An experience that most of the parents will, sadly, never have had. That is how you break the cycle, how you bridge the attainment gap and how you actually 'level up'. It is how families are re-engaged in education. If we are not here to break the cycle, what are we here for? The politicians can argue about the big issues, but the real work is done face to face with families. It starts with giving. Giving until they are compelled to give back.

Relationships are therefore essential. They are the foundation for an ambitious and high-performing school. Not relationships that are just on the school's terms, but relationships that form a familial bond. When the school is part of the family, everything changes for the child.

I learned about relationships from my very first teaching job. I was an early career teacher, but I didn't learn it from the hours I spent in the classroom. I learned it through coaching school sports, after-school clubs and local sports clubs. By building trust through play, by being outside playing cricket every break and lunchtime and running after-school activities, I developed relationships that had real strength and depth. Relationships where mutual respect flourished. From Monday to Friday I ran five different sporting clubs – football, cricket and skipping (yes, I taught double Dutch!). And on Friday nights in the summer I coached at the local cricket club in the village.

I have carried what I learned from coaching those teams in the early days throughout my career. I saw how children developed and flourished with positive reinforcement. I learned how to get the best out of them by constantly reminding them of the finest elements of their play. I was handing out positive carrots – and they kept coming back for more. They carried that positivity and favourable self-image into games and back into the classroom.

When it came to being a head teacher, my focus was on bringing the whole team together in a similar way – office staff, learning mentors, teaching assistants, kitchen staff, caretakers, everybody. Everyone on the same team and everyone on the same bus. To do that, we needed to be able to play together as well as work together.

Safeguarding is Love

We got wind that a child hadn't eaten. Lunch was the first meal he'd had that day. He was a lovely lad. We brought him into my office. If he had asked we would have got him some bagels or extra breakfast, but it is hard to ask. It is hard to admit you are hungry. Children feel shame just as acutely as adults. Food poverty is understandable: people go hungry because their pride stops them from speaking up. It is difficult for some teachers to imagine being that hard up. Few who make it through to the teaching profession will have experienced hunger as a child. You learn to be humble in the face of such poverty.

We were able to react straight away. We gave the family money to go to a supermarket and buy some food for tea that day. We made sure the child had a carrier bag of food to take home as well. No fuss, no drama, no embarrassment. Isn't that what anyone would do if they discovered that someone they loved was going hungry? That is what is needed. That is Parklands. We noticed something we could do something about, and we made it right.

At Parklands, we don't chase up debt arrears on lunch payments. If parents are in trouble and a bill is due, we will write it off. If lack of food is a barrier to learning, we will deal with the problem at source.

We have some children who are struggling through really difficult situations – anything from a family member in prison to a parent with a terminal illness, from domestic abuse, drug addiction or neglect to simply running out of money. It is vital to have highly trained, designated staff who are experienced in supporting families who are suffering. At Parklands, I am blessed to have a team who share my ethos and values.

Legally, all staff must update their Child Protection Certificate every three years. We do it every two years, and we are constantly training staff, and reviewing and interrogating our procedures. As the great Paul Garvey observes, curriculum is king but safeguarding is queen.[2] Safeguarding is always at the forefront of our minds. Love and safeguarding go hand in hand.

Developing relationships where children feel valued and respected means they will speak openly to staff. Children will often disclose to individuals they trust about events that are going on in their home lives. We never encourage it; they just know they are safe when they are with us. People tend to be more candid when they realise they will be listened to. Children recognise when they find a safe space and a safe adult. We train our adults in how to manage these disclosures, how to record and refer and, most importantly, how to make sure the child knows that none of it is their fault. They are not to blame – and they need to hear it.

Our staff are unshockable and understand the importance of how an adult reacts to a disclosure. Being highly effective in safeguarding means they are able to control their reactions. If they appear to be shocked by what a child is telling them, the child is likely to feel worse and say less.

---

2   Paul Garvey, *Taking Control 2: How to Prepare for Ofsted Under the Education Inspection Framework* (Carmarthen: Crown House Publishing, 2020), p. 30.

Our response is always to listen, not to judge or blame, and never to suggest anything to the child. Listening without prejudice is a skill that can be taught. It is critical that in their most vulnerable moments children are treated with the utmost respect. It is not easy to tell an adult about things you might not understand yourself.

Meeting and greeting is a valuable way to identify the daily needs of the children first thing in the morning. When you are meeting and greeting every child on their way into school, you notice so much that is useful. Often, you know which children you are looking out for – the children who are coming in angry or cross, the children who have just seen their dad beat up their mum, the children who haven't eaten, the children who have already had a traumatic morning of arguments. It is all about being well-informed about your pupils. If you love them you will know them really well. Safeguarding is not simply about policy and process. It is also about noticing small details and small changes. It is about being there when a child wants to talk. It is about being slow to judge when their struggles come to the surface in other ways, usually through their behaviour.

Exam results are great. Business money coming into school is great. Small class sizes are great. But nothing is more important than safeguarding. A safe school, built on love, is one where teaching and learning don't have distractions. Disruptions to learning are as rare as a blue goldfish at Parklands. Violence, bullying and fear are dealt with straight away with a robust plan. We do not allow our pupils to be discriminated against.

It is imperative that we stay connected with our pupils over the summer break. We open up the school for two days a week all through the summer holidays. We want to make sure that everyone gets a couple of really good hot meals (breakfast and lunch) twice a week and to experience a day out. It is part of our safeguarding plan. Otherwise, many would be stuck on the estate for the six-week holiday with no support.

We also identify vulnerable children. We have a child protection list which determines live cases, but underneath there are still many other vulnerable children. The families are on our radar. All of our summer activities are geared towards these children. It gives the parents a break too. We say to them, 'On Tuesday and Thursday this week we're going to Flamingo Land and the Northern Ballet. It won't cost you anything. Just make sure they're at school at 9.30am.' The parents love it: 'Brilliant. We can't afford to take them there – they're all yours!'

While we were at the Northern Ballet in 2020 (*BBC Look North* came down and filmed it!), one of the kids was complaining, 'Oh, my arm's killing me.' I asked her how long it had been hurting (it was a bit swollen), and she said, 'Since last week – I fell out of a tree.' We were in the city centre and Leeds General Infirmary was only five minutes away, so we popped down to the hospital with her. She had a broken arm. Luckily, this was the third week of the summer holiday, but if we hadn't had that child on that amazing experience, then her injury might not have been picked up. We are not social workers knocking on doors: 'Right, we need to see your children to make sure they're alright!' We organise summer activities so they can stay connected to Parklands and so we can check in with them. Interestingly, the parents hadn't done anything to contribute to the child's broken arm; she had just fallen out of a tree. Kids climb trees.

Summer activities are a nice way to keep in touch with the most vulnerable families. Many of our parents dislike social workers. We are equally as concerned, but we are able to connect in different ways. The staff love volunteering for summer activities because it gives them overtime for two days a week and is extra money in their pocket.

In Leeds, we are blessed to have Raminder Aujla, the education and early years safeguarding team manager at Leeds City Council, who is probably the nation's leader when it comes to child protection and safeguarding. We have our own designated hotline for child protection and maintain a really close relationship. The support of the local authority is invaluable. Each cog turns another. We are very proud of our safeguarding work. In partnership with every outside agency, we make sure that families and children don't slip through the net.

Mrs George

There weren't many teachers who 'got me', but Mrs George was different. I was 7 years old. Mrs George was like Miss Honey from Roald Dahl's *Matilda*. She always had a smile for me. I remember once having an embarrassing accident in the toilet. Soon after, I could hear the head teacher on the warpath trying to find out who had made such a mess. I kept out of the way, but Mrs George knew it was me. I heard her telling the head, 'Kids don't want to be humiliated when they have accidents. No one deliberately has an accident in the toilet.'

She just came and sat with me. She was the first person who understood me. The first person who knew I was a bit hyper and had a bit too much to say. But she showed me compassion anyway. I learned a lot from Mrs George, and she had a great impact on the sort of teacher I became. She taught me that you get the best out of people through kindness as opposed to threatening them with a stick.

I needed things to be explained to me. I used to get the cane or ruler for getting subtractions wrong, when I just needed someone to show me how to do it. Mrs George was the teacher who explained it, modelled it and showed me the way with patience and love. I carry her example with me every day. Here, at Parklands, I have a team of Mrs Georges working and inspiring the children.

Pastoral and Welfare Teams

Our pastoral and welfare teams are a critical link between home and classroom. They remove barriers to learning for children and families every day. From helping parents to establish morning routines at home to intervening with behaviour and working with the class teacher, the pastoral teams work behind the scenes to make sure the children are ready to learn. In a very practical sense, our staff might be having a cup of tea in the family home in the morning and sitting alongside the child in class in the afternoon. The pastoral and welfare team also provide play therapy, run nurture groups, organise grief counselling and deliver workshops on tricky issues such as domestic violence. They are an essential part of the Parklands fundamentals.

On an estate like Seacroft, life expectancy isn't as high as it is in wealthier areas. Sadly, a few parents have passed away since I have been at Parklands. I, or a member of the senior leadership or pastoral team, will attend the funerals. It is important that someone is there on behalf of the school. It can be really tough, but sometimes in the middle of the sadness and solemnity, a child will realise that one of us is there and utter a cry of 'Hello! Yay!' It breaks the tension beautifully.

I remember the first parent who died. I was over in Scarborough on holiday when I heard. I drove from Scarborough to a Tesco in Leeds and picked up £200 worth of shopping. I dropped it off at the family's home so there was plenty of food in the house. I wanted to let them know that we were thinking of them, that Parklands was there for them. I then returned to Scarborough, knowing how lucky I was to have my family waiting for me. We are a school built on love. There are no limits to it.

I say to all the children who move on at the end of Year 6, 'When you leave that door never closes, it never shuts. You will have issues at high school, so come back and see us. We are always here for you.' On training days, we regularly get a majority of the children who have just left coming back into school to say hi and check in with us. That is the best testimony and what you want from a school.

Parklands Fundamentals

- Make the children the most important thing. Make it obvious. Create the conditions for love to grow.

- Reach out to the community and be ready to make all the moves.

- Accept that some people will say no. Never give in.

- Relationships are two-way. The more you give and the more you value people, the more they give back.

- Break the cycle. The reputation of the school within the community is critical.

- Be brilliant at safeguarding. Go over and above.

I have worked with both Ronaldos, Wayne Rooney, Ronaldinho, Zinedine Zidane, but none of them have left an impact on me like the children at Parklands.

Colin Nell, professional football freestyler

Chapter 2
Leadership

Chapter 2
Leadership

I remember my first assembly with the staff and children as head teacher. I promised that we would make Parklands the best school in the world within four years. Some colleagues rolled their eyes. I don't blame them; they had heard it all before.

Leading a great school means using your personality and your strengths and creating a niche for yourself. The advice leaders often get is to be hard early on, to be firm, don't joke, don't smile until Christmas – all of that nonsense. I never did any of that. I wanted to go in, meet the community and get them onside. Do it the right way.

But not everyone has to be as loud and as over the top as I am! There are many leadership personalities that work differently and perfectly.

I have watched Simon Smith, the head teacher at East Whitby Academy, deliver the most incredible, reflective assembly during which the children were utterly absorbed. Simon's strength is picture books and he works it magnificently. He can draw in children and infer the most amazing meaning without jumping up and down or bursting into a guitar solo (as I do!).

Alternatively, you might create the most wonderfully creative school, like Melanie Cox has at Gomersal Primary School, where art is the way in. You might be like Mark Unwin over at Frank Field Education Trust in Lancashire or Nikkie Beniams at Knayton Church of England Primary Academy, who are both brilliant at developing writing through the curriculum. It is so important to use your niche and your strengths as a leader. It is *your* starting point and *your* specialism. Use it, work it; it will give you better results than following someone else's leadership prescription.

My forte was maths, particularly times tables. It made sense that I chose to make it my first initiative at Parklands. It was my way of showing everyone that children from Seacroft can achieve as well as anyone in the country.

I lead, and have always done so, from the classroom. I am a teacher who wants to stand alongside their colleagues, not to stand in judgement over them. There are times when being a head teacher means making difficult, lonely choices, but that is a small aspect of the job. I am part of a team and most of my time is spent with the team. There is no 'them' and 'us' here. A them-and-us culture created by poor leadership poisons any idea of teamwork. It creates unnecessary tension and takes energy away from working with the children.

In my early days at Parklands, I was even more hands-on. I would be in and out of classrooms, team teaching, demonstrating, modelling and showing the pedagogy I wanted to encourage. Those early days were so important in setting the climate. People saw that I could teach, that I wasn't just a leader in a shiny suit occupied with 'more important' things. I was leading from the front using everything I knew to shape the pedagogy and cultivate a genuinely collegiate feel for the adults. A teacher leading teachers, not a spreadsheet manager or a half-baked visionary.

For me, what makes the difference is being able to walk the walk in front of your colleagues and set the standard while teaching their classes. The children soon understand what the expectations are and see that they are shared. The head teacher doesn't have to be the best teacher in the school, but leading by doing the job is highly effective, particularly in a primary school. It saves endless meetings and training sessions where you chew over possible ways forward. It is live and direct, every day, until the standards are embedded.

The common language and shared understanding and experience is professional development where and when it matters most – in the classroom. It is so much easier to answer questions by demonstrating the effect of new techniques on the children there and then. The more embedded standards, expectations and routines become, the less I need to jump into a teaching role. (But colleagues will tell you that I still can't resist it, especially if there is a cupboard I can spring from and get involved!)

Leading by teaching is the simplest form of leadership. The discussions with colleagues that it promotes are always rich and the children are always the focus. Teachers prefer to be shown how to do things rather than be told how to do them. A teacher observing for 30 minutes in a classroom of 30 children can be more valuable than 30 INSET days where everything is discussed in theory but rarely shown in practice. Today, eight years into the journey, the success of succession planning means that our teachers are now taking on the role of modeller because they are the inspirational experts from whom new staff can learn. Empower your teachers to be leaders and sharers!

Tig on the Roof

When a new head teacher comes in you have got a choice – stick or carrot. I went for the vegetarian option. In the year before I became the head there had been around 150 fixed-term exclusions, which was a record high. Staff morale was on the floor; there was a 33% mobility rate of teachers coming in and out of the school. Despite money being poured into training, the school was stuck. There were heavy sanctions but behaviour was getting worse.

Tig (or tag) on the roof was a very popular game before I started. There would often be six or seven pupils running around on the flat roof next to reception for most of lunchtime. Not the safest place to be and not the best advert for the school. Below them, the head teacher, deputy head and behaviour support worker would be alternately begging, cajoling and threatening the children. None of it worked. The children ignored them. I resolved that this would not happen on my watch.

On my first day I told the children, 'Right, if anyone goes on the roof now, nobody is going to come out after you. You won't have a crowd of staff to play to. I will call the police, and they will come and get you down.' Within about 20 minutes, one child was on the roof; 15 minutes later, a riot police van turned up, two coppers jumped onto the roof of the van and dragged the child down. All the cheering from the corridors turned to silence as they watched the police officers escort the child into the van, sirens on and down to Elland Road station. Nobody has been on the roof since then.

Early on in that first term, I pulled together all the children from the previous year who had been excluded for playing tig on the roof and a variety of other lunchtime, ahem, indiscretions. Using our pupil premium funds, I gave them a real cheque for £10,000 and said, 'Here's £10,000 – design your own playground. You can have whatever you like – so long as it's not a swimming pool!' The children wanted adventure climbing walls or an assault course because our kids love physical play. There are some children who can do front flips straight off the top of a climbing frame and land perfectly. Absolutely fantastic street gymnasts. They chose to build two football pitches and a basketball court; they invested the money really well. This had a huge impact on lunchtimes because the pupils wanted to be out playing as opposed to having nothing to do and therefore causing mischief.

Inclusive Leadership, Leading Inclusion

In some schools inclusion is a small part of the business of education. At Parklands it is a central value and takes many different forms.

If we teach with love, then inclusion is our starting point, not our ambition. We teach the children in front of us, not the ones who are easier or less raggedy or more secure or more perfect. We teach our community, not one that is selected by exam or behaviour or uniform. These are the children who need us, the ones for whom we need to bridge the achievement gap. Schools shouldn't be allowed to curate their own cohorts in order to appear better than they are.

Leading with integrity means understanding that inclusion is an advantage, not a limiting factor. Working alongside children who are different is part of our education at Parklands. It is a privilege to be taught in an inclusive school. It isn't second best. It represents the building blocks for an inclusive society. The school must be at the heart of the community that surrounds it. Anything else is just gaming the system. Play the cards you are dealt, and play them as best as you can. You don't get to swap the cards in your hand, even when the stakes are high and people tell you, 'Those kids can't make it.'

I remember Mr Bentley – he was a teacher you don't forget. He was real old school and really hard. If he spoke to you, you were in trouble. I remember once when my football went over the playground fence. I asked, 'Please can I go and get my football?' Predictably, he said no. I said, 'It's only there. I can see it.' 'I said *no*,' he responded. Regardless, I ran off, grabbed the football and threw it back in. 'Come here,' he hissed. I walked slowly towards him, and he slapped me in the face with the back of his hand. I still remember the stinging pain. 'If I say no, it means no,' he growled.

When we built a school based on love, these were the types of experiences that drove me. Nobody is going to be treated like that physically or emotionally at Parklands. Every child has the right to be safe and deserves to feel secure, even if their behaviour, like mine, sometimes falls short.

Uniform

Parklands was once a school where hardly anyone wore a uniform. The jumpers were too expensive and when one was lost nobody could afford to replace it. The uniform wasn't uniform; it was just another visible demonstration of poverty. What the uniform advocates don't realise is that uniform doesn't hide deprivation. When you are wearing a threadbare jumper that has been handed down four times already, a uniform doesn't feel much like an equaliser.

The old school uniform also included badges which added to the cost. Branded uniforms might look good on a policy document. They might even look good on the balance sheet, as many schools get kickbacks from uniform suppliers. But it doesn't feel good if you are a parent arguing with the school about being unable to afford it. Introducing branded uniforms into areas of poverty is just another way to exclude poor families. Sorry, Jesus, no sandals.

An insistence on logos on uniforms doesn't work for our families. It becomes yet another barrier to achievement. We have had kids in PE with no trainers because parents can only afford one pair of shoes. Imagine, in that context, announcing that everyone has to spend £60 or £70 on a pair of new shoes or that the children will be sent home for wearing a polo shirt without a logo. We are trying to reach out to our community, not push them away.

The uniform was a clear obstacle for some families, so we changed the policy. Now, everything can be bought at a supermarket for a quarter of the price of the uniform shop. It was one of the best decisions we ever made. You can buy a jumper for £3 at Asda or a pair of trousers for £5 at Tesco. What difference does the colour of your socks make to anyone's learning? What difference does having brown or black shoes make?

I feel gutted when the children go to high school and have to wear an expensive blazer. It costs £70 because it has the school badge on it. Socks, shoes, haircuts – does any of it make an impact on achievement? No. If you love someone, why would you care if they were sporting a logo? Love is not conditional at Parklands. It is inexplicable why some schools seem more obsessed by how children look than how well they learn.

Behaviour

If you get the behaviour right, teachers can take risks. Teachers can teach the most flamboyant lessons knowing the children are going to manage their excitement and stay engaged. Children start having stimulating, enriching lessons and going home happy. And if the children are going home happy, then the parents are supportive. It is a simple cycle to express on paper but much harder to achieve in practice. However, when you get all these key ingredients right, you create a successful school. It all starts with behaviour.

Some children need help to manage, understand and articulate their emotions. Children who find it most difficult to conform to 'good behaviour' need to be treated with respect and made to feel valued. Effective teaching and learning is dependent upon positive relationships between staff and pupils, as well as peer-to-peer relationships. It is essential that staff are consistent when enforcing the school rules with high expectations and will challenge unacceptable behaviour with a solution-focused response: one that seeks to move forward, not simply apportion blame. At Parklands we have rooted our policy in an overwhelmingly positive approach towards managing behaviour. The policy is based on incentives and golden rules; when required, sanctions will be enforced. The success of our policy will not be tested by the absence of problems, but the way in which we deal with them.

Parklands behaviour policy

When I arrived at Parklands, the teachers feared taking risks because behaviour problems would accelerate quickly. It was better to play it safe. The foundations for great behaviour weren't in place. I told the staff that we had a lot to change, but we didn't try to build Rome in a day. I knew they had already done a huge amount of in-service training, and also I knew how little impact it had made. I understood that I needed to work on behaviour first but not with endless training sessions. The senior leadership team (SLT) and school improvement adviser agreed with me.

One of the first things we did was to ban shouting. We wanted things to be calmer immediately. I also wanted the adults to be slower to judge, to take more time and care, and for kindness to flourish. You can't have that and have shouting too. We praise loudly and grizzle softly at Parklands. You won't hear a raised voice in our school, unless it is someone exploding with joy or an overenthusiastic voice belting out 'Sweet Caroline' in assembly. Banning shouting is a simple way to change a lot of adult behaviours that don't help. It lets the children know that things are different here, and it sends a powerful message to parents: when adults are in control they don't shout. Adults at Parklands are so in control of themselves and their work that they don't need to shout. Many of our children experience the opposite at home. We never want to remind them of that in school.

Under the old system, the head had a different view about how to deal with behaviour. Pupils would be sent out of the classroom to an exclusion room. This room was where every dysregulated child wanted to be – it was party time! Seventeen of the wobbliest children and just one teaching assistant. There were plenty of opportunities for even more poor behaviour in the exclusion room. There was a CCTV screen in the head's office where you could watch chairs being thrown around. It was a complete riot.

At 2pm each day, the deputy head, behaviour support worker and council support worker would go into the exclusion room, randomly select a child and put them in the padded cell. Children would also be pinned down by staff in the corridors and classrooms using restraint techniques in which they had been trained. (I had an older brother and knew there was nothing worse than being pinned down.)

The stick was dominant throughout the school; the carrot was nowhere to be seen (not even a distant whiff). This punitive approach was having no positive impact on behaviour whatsoever. In fact, it was simply making things worse. Relationships between staff, children and parents were at an all-time low, the behaviour data was drifting in the wrong direction and exclusions were through the roof. So we flipped it.

We didn't start with love. We started with positive behaviour. A transformation needed to take place but it required some planning. In that very first staff meeting, we talked about how the school had had four different behaviour policies because there had been four head teachers in the previous year. Everyone recognised the chaos that had resulted. There was no consistent response to poor behaviour. Most measures were reactive and there was very little proactive work. We were putting out fires metaphorically and sometimes literally.

Leadership churn can be so destructive in a school. The parents, kids and teachers didn't know if they were coming or going. We needed a period of true stability so that a new culture could grow. We decided that the adults had to write and own the behaviour policy. They were the people in the classrooms, they knew what was needed and they had experienced everything that hadn't worked.

For us, it was about being consistent with the children – having simple rules and being really clear about rewards and consequences. The staff wanted a straightforward system. We settled on green for all good; if a pupil was placed on orange they would go next door to another teacher for 20 minutes to reflect and to continue with their work and then return; if things escalated then the child would be moved to red and either I or the SLT would deal with them.

One of the useful pieces of feedback we got from staff was that they didn't feel the previous leadership team had supported them with behaviour issues. When you feel helpless, behaviour problems spiral. I never wanted to leave people feeling unsupported. I wanted them to know that if a child was on red, then it would be dealt with immediately. Even in that first year, we still had to administer some fixed-term exclusions (on around 12 occasions for two days at a time). As the new culture and climate grew throughout the year, it dropped from 12 to one to zero. As trust and relationships blossomed, sanctions became less and less important. Eventually, they were used so infrequently that a child would rarely get to red.

Our approach to behaviour was built on rewards. It was the rewards that changed the behaviour and turned it all around. The consequences were not a true deterrent. They simply allowed us to identify those children who needed help and to make sure they got support, fast. Just as we pride ourselves on our same-day interventions in maths, so we put great store in our swift interventions for behaviour.

The rewards were represented by a ladder. Pupils started on green, but everyone could move up the ladder: silver was 'doing the right things, impressing' and gold was 'excellent behaviour and perfect role model'. It wasn't, and isn't, more complicated than that. The complex bit is working out what support the child needs in order to change their behaviour. The system itself is simple, personal and utterly consistent.

At first the children wanted sweets as rewards. I know that doesn't fit with what we know about healthy eating, but I also remember as a child never having the money to buy sweets. For many of our children, school provides most of the food they eat. We offer great healthy meals, but we also allow the children some of the treats and nice extras that other children might get as a matter of course. Your school community might need something different. Our pupils wanted fast food, football cards and reading books. They had total choice over their rewards.

My experience has been in tough areas, so I am sharp on behaviour. But I have always treated the children with respect and expected their behaviour to be of a high standard. Our standards are firm, clear and demonstrated to everyone – staff and pupils alike. In this way, responses to behaviour also become predictable for everyone. The children love the love we show them, they are excited by the rewards and they don't like it when we have to give them a coldish shoulder because of their choices.

Save yourself the eight-hour INSET day and get into classrooms to adjust the behaviour to your requirements. It might just be the fastest way to establish the consistent practice that makes behaviour easy for everyone to support. As I write this, eight years down the line, the behaviour in our school is outstanding in each and every class. It is simply part of the Parklands fundamentals.

We got our school council going straight away too. They helped us to shape the policy and provided a child's perspective. They also gave us input on consequences and rewards. That was the first task – real collaboration with the people who matter. We then got the parents into school to share the policy with them and to describe our expectations.

School rules agreed with staff and school council:

- Be cool – walk in school.
- Look after our school – don't be a fool.
- Use quiet voices – not silly noises.
- Wear your uniform with pride – have the team on your side.
- Be ready to learn – don't take the wrong turn.
- Play safe together – whatever the weather.

We started with positive behaviour and deliberately catching children doing the right things. We tightened the consistency, improved the way we responded to behaviour and all got on the same page. The team came together. While we were busy working on our skills in managing behaviour, the children were falling in love with their school again. Don't underestimate the impact of this. Suddenly, everyone was pushing in the same direction and the behaviour of the children was changing too. The culture began to shift, relationships were blossoming and learning conversations overtook behaviour conversations. Everyone started to believe in their school and in their brilliant teachers and teaching assistants.

I remember playing 'Ho Hey' from the Lumineers at the beginning of an assembly. The lyrics mention love and sweethearts a lot. I thought it was great because the music made an immediate positive difference. It has a lovely melody and the children, instead of winding each other up, were coming into assembly singing.[1]

---

1   See https://www.youtube.com/watch?v=zvCBSSwgtg4

I belong with you, you belong with me

You're my sweetheart

Love, we need it now

Let's hope for some

'Cause, oh, we're bleedin' out.

It is a song about unrequited love but the children just loved it for itself. Each time we played it they sang with more confidence and started creating moves to go along with the words. I put the lyrics on a big screen and when the words came up, the kids would make love hearts with their hands. Staff used the sign too. It was the first time the word 'love' had been hinted at, but it remained unspoken. The children had found a sign they were comfortable using and which made it easy for everyone to express their love for their 'new' school. When I walked the corridors, I would use the same sign to put people in a happy place. It became our thing. It still is.

When a school is built on love, then alongside behaviour policy and practice something else is in play too. The children know that we love them. When they behave poorly and need to be spoken to, they are worried that we will be disappointed. We don't need to raise our voices, threaten tons of bricks or plan a series of punitive sanctions. There is a strong bond between us already. They know and appreciate what the school has done for them. We always remind them of their successes, even in the most difficult moments.

Leading By Being There

It sounds odd, but there is a simple truth about school leadership. If you aren't there enough, it doesn't work. There are so many opportunities for leaders to be out of school – all seemingly good reasons – important courses, vital meetings, apparently essential conferences. Quickly, a head teacher can find themselves out of school for a day a week, perhaps two. Couple this with an office door that is closed, and in some schools the children don't really know who the head teacher is (and sometimes the staff too!).

Start from the idea that, as the leader, you will be in school every day. Resist those tempting courses and networking opportunities, the sandwiches with the crusts cut off and cheese and pineapple hedgehogs. Refuse the day-long conferences, relocate the meetings that are seemingly vital to your office and be in and among it every day.

During that first 18 months, I had a hand in everything. I produced all the school improvement plans, action plans and policies. There was so much that I didn't want to let go of that it took me a while to see that we had middle leaders who were straining to take on more responsibility. Now, the SLT and I work on the school improvement plan together and then they implement different elements of it. Instead of me doing everything, I now have a solid team with total autonomy.

We have the best deputy head teacher (and I mean the best) and SLT that we could ever have dreamed of. In addition, two colleagues have gone on to become specialist leaders in education, so they go out and help other schools. I used to lead by teaching model lessons. I don't need to do this any more because my staff are now better teachers than me. Losing the crown of being the best teacher in school is to be embraced when you empower a team who can go to the next level.

Parklands Fundamentals

▪ Compassion, inclusion, integrity and availability. Treat people in the way you would like to be treated to get the best out of them.

▪ Communicate love in a way so that everyone feels comfortable.

▪ Leading with love means that behaviour comes first. You don't have to rule with an iron fist to get results.

▪ Start with positive behaviour that grows into love and trust – and the results will follow, academically and emotionally.

▪ Build your own meritocracy with staff – based on skills, not age.

▪ Play the deck you have been dealt – children and colleagues.

▪ Lanyard on, always. #Standards.

The school is ... not just a school; it is a hub for the community. The staff are showering the children with kindness. Kindness may even be too weak a word; 'love' is more appropriate.

Paul Taylor, former principal, Fulneck School

Chapter 3
Learning

Chapter 3
Learning

I remember a visit to Parklands before I was appointed when I had to be careful about walking into a classroom. I had no idea what would be thrown towards the door. I watched as staff would hesitate outside classrooms, knock, wait, cough, open the door and quickly duck before entering. It wasn't good.

Then there were the classrooms where the children were quiet and seemingly well-behaved. Classrooms where you could hear a pin drop. It turned out they were colouring in – all lesson. When I asked a member of staff why, she said, 'We couldn't get the children to do any work in the afternoons, so now we just give them colouring. It's better that way.' It must have seemed like the longest of afternoons for the staff and children. This seemed to happen every afternoon too. The children's behaviour was dictating the adults' behaviour. Everything was upside down and needed to be turned up the right way.

When you get the behaviour right, the learning bites and time just flies by. Tasks that simply occupy children are of no benefit to anyone. They might appear to ease the teacher's headache for an hour or two, but the effect on the culture is devastating. It sends all the wrong messages. Children are in school to learn. The adults need to sustain high expectations and create an environment for the children to learn. Dumbing down the curriculum for an easy life is cheating the children of their potential. It is the worst kind of compromise.

A bored child is frequently a disruptive child. I was never top of the class when I was at school. I was always in a bit of bother, often in detention. I missed playtimes and was on the receiving end of many stern words. The truth is I was bored. I know that if I'd had a colouring pencil in my hand all afternoon, needlessly doing hours' worth of colouring in, then when the teacher wasn't looking the pencils would have been launched across the room.

When I visited Parklands before being offered the job as head teacher, I saw wall displays splattered with ink from where pens had been thrown. The children would lob them across the room and play the game of 'it wasn't me' when the teacher turned round. That was going to stop as soon as I was in post. I had higher expectations. They were going to learn in the afternoon. It would be the end of colouring in and boring lessons.

The Parklands curriculum is very important to us. It has got to be broad and rich, and it has got to deliver experiences that the children wouldn't normally encounter being from such a deprived area. The school used to be entirely focused on maths, reading and writing. The three R's domi-nated lessons all morning and the afternoons were full of interventions, interventions, interventions, with children being pulled out of class seemingly randomly. There was little strategic planning. Standards were rock bottom, the interventions weren't working and the repetitive, lim-ited curriculum was disengaging children from the learning.

I am a big believer in residential trips. I wanted to make sure that each year group from Years 3–6 had a residential that was closely linked to the curriculum. At Parklands, residential trips are an essential foundation for the curriculum, not a nice add-on. We see the impact these experi-ences have on our children's writing and cultural understanding.

The year 2020 saw the very first Year 3 residential, for which we part-nered with Fulneck School, an all-through independent school in Pudsey. We had the luxury of the Fulneck science department teach-ing our pupils about space and rockets, before the children put on their walking shoes and set off to explore the historic town. In the evening, we camped among 60 acres of magnificent countryside and got to lie down on the grass and gaze at the stars.

Year 4 head off each summer term to the Lake District for three days of adventure. Kayaking, ghyll scrambling and sunset walks are accompanied by restaurant dining and cookouts.

In Year 5, the children spend three days doing a coastal study in the beautiful town of Whitby. They stay within the ruined abbey walls at the flagship youth hostel before doing a wide range of seaside activities, including beach trawls and fossil hunts. In addition, they study the impact Captain Cook had on the British Empire and investigate the town's fishing industry. The children also spend a day with the Royal National Lifeboat Institution, studying the vital role they play in Whitby. And, obviously, the children and staff enjoy jogging up the famous 199 steps to the abbey twice a day.

Year 6 wrap up their Parklands experience with a week-long stay at a PGL centre doing activities aimed at experiencing new challenges and building teamwork. When you have been standing 30 metres high in the sky on the top of a small circular wooden platform, facing the elements, attached to a rope and preparing to take the 'leap of faith', it imprints on the memory. With your heart beating like a drum and your legs turning to jelly, you take a deep breath and a step into the unknown! When you realise you have done it, a smile engulfs your face as you know that your determination has made you the proudest person in the world. After this, you know not just how to describe fear in your writing, but you have also experienced the resilience needed to do something new. This stuff lasts a long time. Our Year 6 pupils absolutely love it.

Outdoor learning works. We are lucky to be on 17 acres of land at Parklands, so we have our own forest school too. Outdoor opportunities for learning, growing and selling our own produce are a vital underpinning for the curriculum.

The constant challenge for our team is what we can do to enhance the learning for the children. Eight years ago, less than 10% of the kids at Parklands had ever been to the seaside, even though Scarborough and Bridlington are just an hour away. For all the reasons that are pulling at your heartstrings right now, we could not allow that to continue.

Our children deserve the very best classroom teaching surrounded by love and high expectations. They also deserve to feel the sand between their toes, to eat an ice cream on the beach and to splash in the sea. No child should grow up without building sandcastles at the seaside. If all you give them is a plastic sandpit, the educational gaps are forever widening. They need experiential learning and cultural experiences to access the learning that others take for granted. Our job is to spot those gaps and to fill them as easily and naturally as possible.

Bridbados!

When we took Year 5 on their residential trip to Whitby, I noticed after being on the beach for a while that there were six girls who were rubbing their toes in the sand and saying, 'Oh, don't that feel funny?' I asked them what felt funny. 'Sand between your toes,' they said. It turned out that, out of the 47 kids we took to Whitby that time, only six of them had been on a beach before. Six! Not just that beach – any beach. That was in 2016. And that was the moment when we decided to put residential trips at the heart of our curriculum.

Now, we shut the school on 18 July and eight coaches take the entire school to the seaside at Bridlington. The coaches are sponsored by local businesses. We have nothing against Scarborough, but we have a free ice cream and parking deal that is irresistible! Bridbados is a very special trip. It brings us together as a school and is a unique and often emotional experience. Seeing children playing on the beach for the first time doesn't feel like work at all, yet it might be some of the best work we do. We organise a coach for the parents too. We all eat fish and chips, play in the sea and savour every moment. We want the very best for these kids.

Sports provision is also important to us. The children love sport and we want to grab that enthusiasm and expand their horizons. We put a lot of money into it, using brilliant people like Bryn Llewellyn and Tagtiv8 (https://tagtiv8.com), Action Mats (www.actionmats.co.uk) and Sports Cool (www.sportscool.org), Rock-iT Climbing (@LazerWarsNE) who do in-house residentials and Commando Joes (www.commandojoes. co.uk) who deliver resilience and team-building work.

We have just signed a deal with the British dodgeball team who use our facilities on a Thursday evening. There are dodgeball hubs around the country and Parklands is now one of them. The kids absolutely adore it. During the pandemic, schools that relied on income from facilities lost a great deal of money. We don't charge our partners for the use of our school buildings. For us, it isn't an income stream but a way of building amazing relationships with inspirational organisations. The payback is always positive for the children.

This arrangement is mirrored with the Pauline Quirke Academy of Performing Arts, who are here on a Saturday – again, totally free of charge. My own daughter goes to the academy over in Bradford. It is a nice middle-class experience at £89 a month. Our parents don't have that sort of money, so we exchange some hall time for two free places for our pupils. They are only too happy to do so, and our children get another opportunity they wouldn't have had otherwise.

We also have excellent links with Northern Ballet, which is the second biggest ballet troupe in the UK. We want our curriculum to be ambitious. We want the children to experience things that would normally be out of their reach. As part of our partnership with Northern Ballet, they hold interviews for new dance teachers for the educational side of their organisation at Parklands. Potential teachers demonstrate their skills with groups of our pupils, and the school council gets to ask a couple of questions as part of the interview panel too. The end result of that is that we get invited to three ballets every year. The performances are inspirational and our children learn so much from the experience. We are not suggesting that every child is going to end up being a ballet dancer, but they might never get the chance to go to a ballet again.

When drama practitioner Sara Allkins had her lessons cancelled by a local high school due to funding issues, we were only too happy to host her drama group (for free). The offer was a godsend for Parklands because it has benefitted not only our children but also our community. Sara encouraged every child and brought out their confidence, which also attracted the attention of Space2 (https://space2.org.uk) and Boff Whalley from Chumbawamba.

Boff went on to write a play/musical called *Oh! I Do Like to Be Beside the Seacroft*, which was staged at the West Yorkshire Playhouse (now the Leeds Playhouse). The show featured four adults in the main parts and children in every other role. Parklands provided 80% of the cast. Such was the demand they had to do two shows which sold out on both nights.

Throughout the project, Sara worked brilliantly with our pupils who rehearsed after school and at weekends. In addition, the children spent two days rehearsing at the Playhouse and learned so much from working in a professional environment. *BBC Look North* came to film the rehearsals. Performing on one of the biggest stages in Yorkshire was an incredible experience for the children.

Mosque and Crisps

Having a curriculum that has real experiences at its core is not always as uncontroversial as going to the seaside. When the pupils are studying Islam, it is important for them to visit a mosque. Simple. The first time I announced that we intended to take the children to a mosque, in 2015, I had more parents outside my door complaining than ever before. It is precisely the reason why we need to take children to different places of worship. Good education erases prejudice – and there is work to be done on an estate where Islamophobia is easily stoked by the far right. What the children learn they take back home, and slowly understanding grows.

In the first year, out of 45 kids who could have gone to the mosque 30 of them signed up. I had about 15 parents to work on, and I spoke to them all.

'They are not going to a mosque!' It was a Friday afternoon, and I said, 'Right, I'm not having you all in here together. You can each have a 10-minute slot.' I was in my office patiently talking to a procession of parents from 3.30pm to 6.10pm. Conversations would typically go:

'It's all part of their education. It's a really important part of the curriculum.'

'They aren't going – they're Christian.'

'When was the last time you went to church?'

'I haven't been to church.'

'It's important. We've got to understand different religions. We've got to experience different cultures. It's totally up to you if your child doesn't go, because they can legitimately drop out of RE, but it would disappoint me because I'm also putting on a Bridlington trip. We are organising lots of free trips, and what I don't like is people who pick and choose what their child attends. You either want the full education package or you don't. Have a think about it over the weekend.'

On Monday morning, I sent a new letter home with the children that read:

> I have slightly changed the trip. We are going to the mosque, leaving school at half-past nine. We are going to the mosque until 11 o'clock, then we are going to McDonald's and then we are going bowling in the afternoon. It is your choice as a parent if you want to opt out.

The next day, every letter came back and they were all going. Every single one of those children had the time of their life. That was the only year I had to have such conversations. From 2016 onwards, every parent gave their permission for their child to go without quibbling. Because I communicate with the parents and let them have their say, I don't have an angry mob coming in and screaming at me.

It is important to know your community and make sure that, irrespective of their views, there is always a way around them. You can always unpick problems without falling out with parents, without saying, 'You *will*.' I knew I couldn't say, 'Well, if your child isn't going to the mosque, they aren't going to Bridlington.' However, there is nothing wrong with gently reminding parents of the benefits of attending all school trips.

The mosque visit is an excellent opportunity to dispel myths about Islam, to educate the children about the basic principles and beliefs of the faith, and to break down any cultural or religious barriers that exist between Muslims and the wider community. The children learn about the mosque and what it is used for besides worship; they hear the call to prayer and watch a demonstration of how Muslims pray; they find out about traditional Muslim clothing and have an opportunity to try some on and have their photo taken; they hear the story of how the Qur'an was revealed to the Prophet Muhammad, and how Abraham and Ismail rebuilt the Kaaba and called humanity to perform a pilgrimage to Mecca. The children also learn about similarities between the Abrahamic religions, in order to build bridges based on commonality. Links are made to Jesus, Mary, the Angel Gabriel, Moses, Noah, Adam and many of the earlier prophets and messengers. Throughout the visit, they are encouraged to ask any questions they may have about Muslims or Islam. As an extra treat, the children get crisps, sweets and pop at the end of the outing!

The excursion includes a broad range of activities, and the children come back enriched because they have sampled something beautiful. They don't fear Islam because they have been to a mosque and seen that it is a calm and lovely place to be, and they have been surrounded by kind and generous people. We make sure the children are educated about discrimination at school, so they can identify it when they see it in their community.

SATs and National Testing

Parklands does quite well with national testing. We do exceptionally well in our maths standardised assessment tests (SATs) and in our reading and writing exams at the end of Key Stage 2, but we wouldn't describe Parklands as a 'testing school' in any way, shape or form. We are not successful because we cram.

That is not to say that we don't care about results. In a normal year, after Easter, we shift into test mode and get some practice in for the SATs. If pupils know how to answer questions on a paper, how to get their timings right and get used to an exam environment, then they are going to score higher, which is going to keep Ofsted away from your door. But we are not one of those schools that spends the whole of Year 6 focused on SATs. At Parklands, no other year groups are tested apart from Year 6. (The children barely notice the Year 2 SATs.)

When we got a remarkable overall score in 2017, we had the SATs police (not their official title I am sure!) in the following year to check we were doing everything properly. The children working on the maths paper finished after just 14 minutes. I noticed they had stopped writing and said, 'I'll think I'll collect them up now.' I was told very sternly, 'You don't touch those papers. They get the full 30 minutes, otherwise we'll have to report it.' Watching that clock for the next 16 minutes was absolute agony. When the papers came back, out of 33 children in that year group, one child dropped a mark. Everyone else got full marks.

COVID-19 meant that SATs were cancelled. The direct result is that we had the worst rounders team we have ever had! But there is an upside – let me explain.

Many schools try to cram in lots of test preparation before May. It is full-on exam prep because there is a great deal to cover in a short space of time. The cramming and exam pressure means that everyone is exhausted, so, after the exams in May, to give pupils a release from the bookwork, it is usually rounders, days out and activities weeks. This end-of-year feeling can easily seep into June and July, meaning that, in practice, between April and August, the children are not developing their writing, maths and history topics in the way they could be. No wonder some high schools feel their pupils are a little rusty by the time they arrive in September – they haven't had a regular rhythm of teaching and learning for six months.

Without SATs, the rhythm of learning has changed. The children have been able to work steadily throughout the summer term without the interruption and disruption of external testing. This is of huge benefit to them as they transition to high school, but less beneficial for the school's rounders team.

When I started at Parklands there were six data drops a year, which is standard in most schools. That meant one week out of every six where teachers were just testing. The school's results were still rock bottom, so we decreased it to three data drops, and now we have only two (in January and July). I don't like wasted time – it mounts up. We spend very little time on national tests, but we love mini-tests, quizzes and other fun ways to help embed the children's learning. The demands of external testing and the obsession with data can disrupt teaching and learning. They are apparently designed to be a judgement on teachers, yet the cost is borne by the children. It makes no sense to me to invest so much time and energy in a testing system that damages education as a by-product.

A school built on love should be helping the community, not chasing marks. Of course, the Parklands experience shows that there is another way to raise achievement. One good thing to emerge from the COVID-19 pandemic has been that people are not so obsessed with SATs, phonic scores and healthy eating awards. The pandemic allowed leaders to focus on what the community needed. It was a glimpse of primary schools without testing – and relationships flourished.

Parklands SEND

Children who have additional needs are not unusual at Parklands. Our strategy for special educational needs and disabilities (SEND) is deeply interwoven into our culture. There are things we do for everyone that impact enormously on pupils with additional needs. Our reduced class sizes are important, for example, as is our commitment to mixed-ability classes. We have staff who are highly trained and very confident with a wide range of abilities and needs.

This might be said of many schools, but we make sure that we invest time, resources and money into training for teaching assistants and teachers. Our teaching assistants are the oil that makes the Parklands machine run smoothly. They stay with classes, build incredible relationships and understand individual needs. Such is the importance of continuing professional development (CPD) for teaching assistants, that our first session this year was delivered solely to this group of staff – the heartbeat of the school. They felt important, empowered and valued.

The success of SEND provision at Parklands is built on persistence, rigour and consistency. We track all SEND interventions carefully to ensure that pupils are making progress. It sounds obvious, yet so many children have had years of intervention and have made no apparent progress. If we find that progress is limited, we review what we are doing, urgently. It is another way in which we prevent time and resources from being wasted at Parklands. The teaching assistants manage this process. We help them to become reflective practitioners who are reactive to the children's changing needs, and never static. The more responsive we are, the quicker we can fill the right gaps.

We have a resource provision base at Parklands for children with an education, health and care plan. It was originally separate from the rest of the school, but this changed in 2017. There is now much more flow between the resource base and the rest of the school, with children attending classes in both places. All the children attend assemblies, as it is much more inclusive. The resource base is linked to SEND provision at the local education authority and places are managed centrally.

Originally, the resource base was for 12 children, but the team who run it are so good that it has now grown to accommodate 21. It was initially designed to offer provision for autistic children, but we now support children with a wide range of needs, including cerebral palsy, severe speech and language difficulties and Down's syndrome.

Parklands Pedagogy

Even though I see myself as a progressive head teacher, a lot of the skills we deploy at Parklands are traditional. For example, our times tables work demonstrates a progressive spin on a traditional approach. The pupils aren't chanting their times tables; they are doing it in a mixed way using Times Tables Rock Stars (see Chapter 4) and other fast-paced interactive games. Competition is used to test one another, not to create a rank order.

The pedagogy at Parklands isn't fixed – we aren't slaves to a single philosophy. We are interested in what works for our children in our community. We will flip different times of the day to different ways of teaching to meet the needs of the pupils. A teacher standing at the front and dictating doesn't work for us. Our children have got to learn how to learn. At primary level, engagement is vital. Creating a positive environment – valuing the children and valuing their answers (no matter how silly) – is absolutely key to successful education.

Our success in maths is part of our niche, but our ambition stretches further than excellence in one area. Following some positive challenge from our governors to lift the passion and results in reading, we have introduced a reading initiative. In Key Stages 1 and 2, the children are expected to read nine different books from a variety of genres. They might try a story from another culture, an autobiography, a poetry anthology, a non-fiction book, a Shakespeare play, a Charles Dickens novel, a pre-20th century novella, some contemporary fiction and a detective story.

We also wanted to put a modern spin on an often-tried reading challenge, so we deployed the awe and wonder of a £200 vending machine (thanks to Rob Smith of EdShed (www.edshed.com)). It is the sort of vending machine you may have seen at your local swimming pools, filled with chocolate bars and crisps. The sort of vending machine where you press A4 only to see your pickled onion flavour Monster Munch edge towards you invitingly and then dangle frustratingly above the collection tray. Slightly snaggy when stocked with lightweight junk food, they work brilliantly with books. Our children win tokens to put in the machine from which they can choose a book to keep. They absolutely love it.

Books are the greatest gift. A vending machine full of books is not just delightful and unusual, it is also essential for our pupils. There are no libraries or bookshops in Seacroft, and many families have no culture of reading. The nearest shops and library are miles away in Leeds. They might as well be on Mars. Outside of the school, most of our pupils won't have bought, borrowed or even seen a book. The excitement on the faces of the kids who get to come out, press D4 and watch their own copy of *Diary of a Wimpy Kid* drop down in front of them brings tears to your eyes. They often ask before they push the tray open, 'Is that for me?' Again, it is so simple, but putting a little twist on it creates some fun and makes it so much more rewarding.

A similar thing happened when we started using Times Tables Rock Stars to put a spin on our times table work. We now have 7-year-olds who can do 160 times table questions in a minute. Children will go further faster once they have been inspired. The amount of effort they put into reading and times tables in their own time is incredible. As a result, they are learning beyond their parents' ability. We use every trick in the book to meet the gap, from providing laptops and devices to Wi-Fi dongles and fabulous software, so they can practise alone or alongside their classmates. We also give them paper, pens and anything else they need.

Make no mistake: underneath all of the strategies to make learning engaging and fun are phenomenally high expectations for the children. If you walked into a classroom at Parklands, you would find a focus that matches any super-strict charter school. We just get there a different way. Our high performance is born from love, not fear.

The high expectations at school extend into the home and are followed up with the highest level of support. Our children are not reliant on their parents to help them with their home learning. The school fills the gap. No child is left behind, regardless of their home circumstances, their starting points or their additional needs.

Literally Flying

Every July we hire a helicopter for the day. I know – that doesn't happen in every school! We always want to do something different. For us, the helicopter is an unmissable annual event.

Every summer, 80 kids get to take off from the school field to fly over York and back. The children who are chosen will have shown that extra bit of resilience when dealing with a tricky situation, gone the extra mile or turned their life around. Or they might have had a death in the family. Honestly, it isn't difficult to find children who are going through genuine difficulties. Not many adults have been on a helicopter ride. It is a wonderful experience. The sensation of being lifted up and seeing the world from a different angle is one that we bring back into the classroom and into our school culture. I can't tell you how great it is! The buzz it generates in the school and in the community is amazing.

The helicopter ride is part of the reward of attending school. Come to school and you will have the chance to fly in a helicopter. Come to school every day (not including authorised absences for medical reasons, family deaths and so on) for your seven years in primary, and you will definitely get to go in the helicopter one year. It is available to everyone. Experiencing something rare and exceptional at school is very special. It feeds into the understanding that being a pupil at Parklands means that they are exceptional too. Yes, remarkable things happen here at Parklands!

Schools may be surprised to learn that the cost of hiring a helicopter is only £750 (including fuel), but be warned that you need an area around the size of two tennis courts in order for one to land. (We are lucky to have 17 acres of school grounds.)

In a place where many families rarely venture further than the shops, the school has a responsibility to create the sort of education the children deserve, to expose them to aspects of life that will pique their interest, and to show them there is a world beyond the estate that is open to them too.

Parklands Fundamentals

- A bored child is a disruptive child. A well-motivated, happy child allows teachers to take risks that will further inspire learning.

- Residential visits should be at the heart of the curriculum. To write about things, you need to experience things.

- There is always a way with parents. Sometimes, they just need a listening ear and someone to whom they can sound off.

- Competition, well managed, is hugely motivating and is an essential life lesson.

- Provide experiences that lift pupils' horizons – helicopter moments!

- Your pedagogy must fit your children and must come from your own soul.

I have seen some brilliant teachers, inspiring classroom environments and many wonderful, motivated children; however, the level of mathematical engagement and understanding I observed at Parklands took my breath away. The numerical fluency at Parklands was simply remarkable.

Simon Kidwell, principal, Hartford Manor Primary School and Nursery and member of the NAHT National Executive

Chapter 4

Fun Day Friday and the Best Seats in the House

Chapter 4

Fun Day Friday and the Best Seats in the House

Fun Day Friday

On Fridays, Parklands turns into the Fun Palace. We call it the Fun Palace, which at first glance might seem at odds with being a high-performing school, but don't worry – we aren't throwing Friday to the dogs every week. Nothing could be further from the truth. Fridays are when the learning and successes from the week are consolidated. It pulls the community together like nothing else. The learning is intense, but nobody even realises it is happening. It is dressed up as fun and everyone loves it. And, more importantly, everyone turns up.

Originally, we decided to give some sparkle to Fridays as a strategy to deter families who might allow their children to have the day off. Friday was the most frequent day for absences when I started at Parklands. Attendance was appalling. We had to turn that around, but doing so with threats, heavy-handed attendance officers and fines wouldn't work at Parklands. It definitely isn't our style and would strain relationships.

Fun Day Friday was the progressive alternative. We had to make sure that Friday was the best day of the week. We had to stop parents allowing their children to take the day off 'Cos it's Friday' or because 'It doesn't matter – it's nearly the weekend anyway'. Almost immediately, the children were unwilling to miss a Friday. Even with some parents wanting to keep them at home, they knew where they preferred to be. Who would want to pass up on a day that was called a Fun Day at a place called the Fun Palace? An idea was born.

Fun Day Friday has grown over the years. There are some essential elements, but it always starts with a sausage sandwich!

Breakfast with the Stars

Fifteen pupils are nominated by the teaching teams as Stars of the Week. Every Friday morning, I get to sit down and spend some time with the children who are going over and above. We eat sausage sandwiches, drink tea and talk about their week. Although you can sense the excitement of the day ahead, it is a quiet and reflective time. They are always full of news, stories and enthusiasm. It is one of my favourite parts of the week. I think that having a spell of time with me as the head teacher is important, although I am sure they would say that the sausage sandwich is the best bit!

Music

Music is central to our Fun Day Friday assemblies, but it is also important to the life of the school. You might be surprised on visiting Parklands that music is played in the hall all day at a fair volume. It flows through the corridors (but not into the classrooms). It creates a unique atmosphere in the school. It would be the first thing you noticed.

As a class teacher, I found a place for music throughout the day. At the start of a maths lesson, I would put on 'We Can Work It Out' by the Beatles, for an English lesson it would be 'Paperback Writer' and for guided reading it would be 'Tellin' Stories' by the Charlatans. It added something distinctive to the lessons. On the back of this, I started to wonder what other music would work well for learning.

In a previous school, everyone had to come into assembly in silence. Even if there was music – and it was mostly Mozart – silence was insisted on. The purpose was to try and get the children to be reflective. It was hard work because it is difficult to connect with children over Mozart. Now, that is not a criticism. Each school is different and, as a teacher, it is essential that you follow the ethos of your school. At Parklands, pop music works well in assemblies; we slip in Mozart at other times.

Exciting school assemblies have so much more potential to bring a community together than silence, long speeches and hard stares from glaring adults. It is almost as if some schools are scared of giving the children a voice. Everything is controlled, dull, forced and false.

I thought we should make the music relevant to the children – although, to be fair, I don't let anyone else touch my playlist! People come up to me all the time and say, 'Put this song on' or 'Put that song on'. I tell them every time, with a smile, 'No, when you become a head teacher you can play whatever you like.'

As the children transition from assembly to lessons, they are often singing quietly or humming a tune. It takes the edge off school life a little and creates a lovely relaxed atmosphere. Music continues to have a huge impact in assemblies and beyond.

On Fun Day Friday the music is a little louder and a lot bouncier. The essential Parklands top 10 assembly playlist is:

1. 'Sweet Caroline' – Neil Diamond

2. 'Think Positive' – Luke Britnell

3. 'Ho Hey' – The Lumineers

4. 'Transylvania' – McFly

5. 'Love Story' – Taylor Swift

6. 'Perfect' – Ed Sheeran

7. 'Fight Song' – Rachel Platten

8. 'Breaking Free' from *High School Musical*

9. 'Count on Me' – Bruno Mars

10. 'Where's Me Jumper' – Sultans of Ping FC

Old School Assembly

I wasn't naughty at school, but I was a show-off. I remember my head teacher asking in assembly whether anyone had watched the FA Cup Final at the weekend. At the time, the Cup Final was a special day for everyone, even if you were watching it on the telly. At home we would be up at the crack of dawn, enjoying the build-up to the match and making a real day of it.

I put my hand up and said, 'I was there, Sir! I was there!' He responded, a little taken aback, 'You were actually at Wembley Stadium?' 'Oh yes,' I said. The trouble was my brother was sitting at the back of the hall, so Mr Wheeler checked in with him. 'Did you go with him?' he enquired. 'No,' said my brother. 'We watched it in the house.' Mr Wheeler pulled me out to the front of assembly and gave me eight whacks of the slipper.

Those whacks of the slipper live long in the memory. The only children coming forward at a Parklands assembly are those who are being celebrated.

He Who Dares ...

On my very first Friday as head teacher of Parklands, I went to M&S and bought 80 doughnuts out of my own money. We had sent a letter and text message to every parent inviting them to the assembly: 'We want you to come into school so we can tell you our dream and vision for the school. We want to tell you what we are going to do with this place. We believe in your children, and we believe in you.'

I piled all the doughnuts in a Ferrero Rocher-style tower of yumminess, and stood at the front door expectantly, excited to greet all the parents and share the dream. Only three parents turned up.

At home time, I dished out the doughnuts to the children and said: 'Listen, I'm going to do this every Friday until I've got 50 parents who are prepared to come and listen to my dreams for our school. Today it felt like my fifth birthday party and nobody came. We are so disappointed.' The following week we had about 60 parents and now at a Friday assembly we get 80 or 90 parents. They come every single week, just to be part of the community.

Getting parents into school is a vital ingredient because if the parents are happy, the children are happy, and we can work together as one. The presence of parents supercharges Fun Day Friday. The afternoon assembly is a community event. We have had to break down barriers. The school must be open for parents, and they need to feel comfortable, welcome and like they belong. We hold three assemblies a week to which parents are invited, and they are all well attended.

In the early days, we needed to give staff some time to work on the behaviour policy and implementation. It was easy to do this if I took the assemblies. They had time to work together and I had time to get to know the children. I had come straight from being a deputy and Year 6 teacher, so I was used to leading large groups and knowing how to get the best out of a team. The children saw me more in that first week – when I was also doing tours around the school – than they had seen the former head teachers in the previous few years.

Best Seats in the House Assembly

The highlight of the week and the place where all competitions, prizes and recognition come together is the Best Seats in the House Assembly (a title we pinched from *Ant & Dec's Saturday Night Takeaway*). It is important that everyone feels a sense of success at the end of a hard week. Parklands' assemblies are more like a game show than a traditional school gathering, and they have featured on many national news channels

61

and in national newspapers. The Friday Best Seats in the House Assembly is now a firm date in the diary for our parents and, most importantly, the children love it.

It is all about celebration, celebration, celebration. If you have ever been to an awards ceremony, the audience doesn't sit there silently. It is an event full of joy and pride, not for personal achievements but for the efforts and accomplishments of others. Our assemblies teach the children to enjoy seeing others succeed. That is a lesson for life. It shows them how to be generous and humble.

At 2pm every Friday, the music is turned up to full volume and the children come into the hall singing and dancing. Some take to the stage like nineties' ravers, others stand up and boogie or throw shapes on the floor and some dance freestyle while seated. If you walked in and didn't know what was going on, it would be easy to assume that either the adults had lost control or you had discovered a secret performing arts school in full flight (think the Kids from *Fame!*). There is community in music, in dancing and in singing together. We shake off the week as one. Even the parents seated on chairs at the back have been known to have a little bop.

When the music finishes, everyone takes their place and is silent and attentive. The pupils are ready to listen in seconds and without fuss. We love having that sort of control because you can let them loose and then draw their attention back immediately. Things are different when there is a deep trust in the room. Our high standards are built on relationships and love, never fear or blind obedience. It is just awe-inspiring when you see it, but our children are willing participants. There is always another way.

We start the assembly by inviting the chosen nine children to sit on the Best Seats in the House. These are the pupils who have gone over and above by bringing in exceptional work they have done at home. The work is placed on the Wall of Love in my office alongside hundreds of other winners.

The Best Seats in the House sofa is set up alongside a snacks table. This is the full VIP treatment. Pizzas are delivered to the table, ice-cold lemonade comes out of the fridge and the selected children settle in. Everyone else is sitting on the floor and singing along to 'Sweet Caroline'. All the pupils are excited for the children in the Best Seats. Who doesn't like to relax in a comfy chair, watch a show, munch on a slice of pizza and sip a cool drink?

The parents sit on chairs at the back of the hall – five or six rows of beaming faces. The atmosphere on Fridays is different to other assemblies. All the staff are in for Best Seats in the House too. They sit at the ends of the rows.

When everyone is seated, the Stars of the Week – still full of breakfast sausage – are called up to receive their certificates. We play 'Shut Up and Dance' by Walk the Moon as their theme tune. Each segment has its own tune or chant, which is a chance for everyone to join in.

Team points are handed out during the week for excellent work. (Every child is allocated to a house team of Ruby, Diamond, Sapphire or Emerald. Older pupils team up with younger children to help create a family vibe.) The team with the most merit points gets to 'dab on that' – to stand up in front of everyone and dab. We take pictures of excessive dabbing and post a photograph of the winning team on the school website. The bouncy castle is also in play as a reward for team points.

Prizes for our Readers of the Week are sponsored by Rob Smith and EdShed (www.edshed.com). The children are chosen by their class teachers and teaching assistants. These pupils are given tokens for the book vending machine. When the tokens are awarded, the children chant: 'Reader of the Week I want to be. Enjoy, enjoy, just like me. Yeah, man!' (Mrs Thackray's Year 4 class wrote this.) Parklands owes Rob and his team eternal thanks for making books accessible to the children who need them the most.

The Writer of the Week is sponsored by Simon Pobble from Hey Pobble. They get their own pencil-shaped certificate and the work is displayed at https://my.pobble.com. The traditional game show-style call and response is 'It's time for this week's ... ' and the children in unison shout 'Writer of the Week!'

Celebrating Punctuality and Attendance

Of equal importance is punctuality, so we also have an award for good timekeeping. It is so important to get to school on time and get the learning underway. At Parklands, we start – five days a week, 36 weeks a year – with our Early Bird Maths (more about this in Chapter 6). We begin learning at 8.50am. The punctuality award is introduced with, 'What do we say?' and the children reply, 'Ten to nine in the line!' (I did magpie this from my previous school, as well as the brilliant Classopoly attendance board game (see below), which shows that great things were happening in those assemblies, despite the Mozart.) The most punctual class each week gets a pass to go on the bouncy castle at the end of every half term to celebrate.

Attendance is everything. It is especially key in deprived areas like ours where there are so many reasons to stay at home. Some families don't see the connection between time away from school and lack of achievement, so we have to be tight on attendance. A day a week or every fortnight has a huge impact on achievement. It breaks the routine for the child, puts them a step behind where they were and makes it all too easy to have another day off.

Our attendance strategy is built on rewards. Any class with 95% attendance gets to play Attendance Classopoly during the Friday assembly. There is delightful tension when the big dice goes up in the air, bounces across the hall – with hundreds of eyes on it – and lands on, say, a 4. We all urgently check to see how this will affect their position on the life-size Classopoly board on the wall and discover what their reward will be. They might win lemonade in the garden, extra ICT time, a turn on the trim trail or even a lesson with Mr Dyson, which goes down quite well.

The absences of pupils who can't get to school because of a medical appointment or a family bereavement aren't counted (we once had a child who was in hospital for four months; they were not included in the figures). We make sure that everything is fair and that children who are unwell are never pressured to attend. Our positive approach to attendance is borne out by the figures: our attendance is 99.8% on a Friday. Nobody wants to be away on Fridays any more. It is interesting how children vote with their feet when the offer at school is irresistible.

Times Tables Grand Final

At Parklands, children can be a times table hero at home by logging on to Times Tables Rock Stars (https://ttrockstars.com), in the classroom in a live duel and in assembly in the Grand Final. This has a huge impact on motivation and confidence in times tables across the school. The Times Table Grand Final, which takes place during the Best Seats in the House Assembly, is sponsored by Times Tables Rock Stars. In front of a huge assembly crowd, the tense final pits the leading times table speed merchants from each class against each other in a face-to-face competition. Like gladiators, the class heroes rise from the floor in assembly and the crowd erupts with support. It is the highlight of the Best Seats in the House assembly. Competitive, intense and utterly compelling. For the build-up to the Times Table Grand Final, we play 'Hard to Handle' by the Black Crowes.

Every child competing in the Grand Final is already a winner. We always make sure they understand, especially the younger children, that if a 7-year-old is playing against an 11-year-old, the younger child has got absolutely nothing to lose. This is critical as we don't want the competitive element to cause an upset. The fact that a 7-year-old is evenly matched against an 11-year-old means they have already achieved great things. We never let them forget that. Each times table hero is already a class champion and, more often than not, it is the 8-, 9- and 10-year-olds who win the overall trophy.

If you have seen any of the footage of our Grand Final, which has appeared on social media, you will notice that everyone is cheering, clapping and supporting one another. When the children announce their name, 'I'm Alfie and I'm representing 4BT,' the entire school cheers and whoops with genuine enthusiasm. (Yes, we allow whooping; if you came along you might whoop too!) What do people cheer for in your school assembly? Do you cheer the children who put in the most effort in their learning?

It is interesting how the children respond to the times table challenge. It is often an equaliser. Children who might not be at the top of the pile initially work hard on their speed. They practise every single night. The bright sparks who know their times tables already perhaps haven't got the rapid response that is required to compete, so they have to work at it too. You will find that if children have worked on them, practised hard and get that love of number, then everyone is performing on a level playing field.

A lot of people ask about the times table competitions, 'Isn't it always the same pupils who win every week?' The truth is that it doesn't work like that. There tends to be a different champion each time. We try to make sure that most children who want to can work to become a class champion at least once during the year. This rebalancing has a huge impact on many of the children who take the responsibility of representing their class very seriously. It is a high honour. And once they get those numbers in their head, they never leave.

Once a week in class, the children can challenge each other to a times table face-off. This isn't as easy as you might think. It might be logical to assume that a classmate who is a little behind on their classwork might be simple enough to pick off in a times table challenge. But, at Parklands, times tables ability doesn't necessarily relate to results elsewhere. Often, a child is challenged and suddenly they reveal themselves to be a secret Times Tables Rock Star and all assumptions about ability are trashed. When Parklands children get the bug for times tables, they get a lot better very quickly.

It began as a times table knockout where there were points for a fancy prize: if you got knocked out in the first round you got one point, in the second round you got two points for winning and if you won the competition you ended up with six points. We would tot up the points throughout the week to find the winner. I bought an England football shirt and whoever was that week's times table champion got to wear the England shirt for the week instead of their school uniform. It caught everyone's attention and provoked their competitiveness. Boys who had never bothered even pretending to like maths suddenly fell in love with numbers. Every child at Parklands grows up knowing that maths is important, rewarding and unquestionably fun.

Baz Winter, who runs Times Tables Rock Stars, is a brilliant friend of Parklands. He organises two Times Tables Rock Wrangle competitions every year (pre-COVID-19) where children compete on a regional level. One is held in London and the other in the North of England. It is like a spelling bee but for maths. The Northern Wrangle is predominantly for children aged 11 and upwards, but we put our 9-year-olds into the competition. Small children were playing against these six-foot 15-year-old youths with beards – and beat them too! The children have nothing to lose and everything to gain.

Healthy competition actually helps to solve behaviour issues. Some of the kids who 10 years ago might have been fighting in the playground to get a feeling of success, now find more satisfaction in being fabulous at times tables than they ever would have got through scrapping.

When we have a spelling bee in assembly, the same feeling of being a hero because of your learning is evident. Coming up to the front and being celebrated as your class Speller of the Week means everything to the children. It has become clear that ability in spelling is not necessarily age related, so these competitions teach humility as well as delivering bragging rights. When relationships are true and trust between children is strong, they give to each other more and more. There is no jeering, only applause. There is no jealousy, only pride. There are no losers. The culture matters here. It takes time and persistence to build it, but when everyone is leading with love the children change.

A highlight of my teaching career at Parklands was during an Ofsted inspection when the inspectors attended a Friday afternoon assembly. At the time, the children were mad for 'Sweet Caroline' by Neil Diamond. In my professional opinion, when you have got three inspectors standing at the back of the hall singing 'Bam, bam, bam', then the inspection might be going quite well! It is impossible not to be moved by a Best Seats in the House assembly. They stick long in the memory for Parklands visitors.

One of the greatest days ever was when Tom Fletcher from McFly tweeted saying, 'At last, our minion army is ready ... ' about a video of the children singing 'Transylvania'.[1] Then, out of nowhere, photos of Best Seats in the House appeared on *Ant & Dec's Saturday Night Takeaway*.

1

Seeing stuff like that makes our day. The children are always delighted by it.

Fun Day Friday and Best Seats in the House assemblies grew slowly over three years. I wouldn't advise launching everything at once; it needs a slower build. We started off with times tables, then introduced Speller of the Week and Writer of the Week celebrations. The music was brought in gradually so that everyone was comfortable with it. It evolved organically, led by the staff and children. The regular appearance of large numbers of parents also helped to make the assembly more celebratory, more performance focused and more game show-like in structure. Other schools have adopted some of our ideas and are doing it their own way. John Bryant at Arthur Bugler Primary School in Thurrock has transformed his Fridays. They are now full of joyful celebrations, including spinning the Wheel of Prizes, Golden Phone Call Home, Hot Chocolate Friday and, of course, Best Seats in the House.

Assemblies at Parklands are part of our whole-school strategy. They are not a 20-minute breather so staff can catch their breath or an attempt to teach silent reflection. They are a full-fat, no-holds-barred celebration of our children and their successes. It is part of the constant reaffirmation that we promote at Parklands – and we can dream big. The Friday assembly creates a positive ripple that reaches through the weekend and into the following week. There is momentum in a celebration that carries everyone with it. Assemblies are culture-building opportunities at Parklands, and we love them.

Parklands Fundamentals

- Fun is not a dirty word. Children learn more and behave better when they are happy, engaged and feel valued.

- Competition can promote positive outcomes for everyone and can raise the biggest smiles.

- Heroes of learning should be celebrated and admired in front of the whole community. Everyone gets to feel that moment of adulation.

- Don't refuse a doughnut – we don't take no for an answer. Every parent needs to attend the Best Seats in the House assembly (99.9% do!). Since lockdown, parents have been most upset that they can't attend assemblies. The social aspect should not be underestimated.

- Music is the beating heart of the school.

- Celebrating as a community builds trust and cements relationships. When you have that relationship, it drives the children on further. Pride works.

The children's enthusiasm grew even more as the 'times table face-off' was due to begin! Firstly, class versus class, followed by the winners of each round, pitted against Tyler in RP [resource provision], who eventually won to the eruption of cheers from his class and polite applause from the rest of the key stage. McFly started up again, as if cheering too, and the children filed out ready for the weekend, everyone smiling and full of love.

Matt Roe, The Leaders Team, Twinkl

Chapter 5
Looking After
Your Staff

Chapter 5
Looking After Your Staff

It seems obvious, but the more you do for the adults, the more they can do for the children. That means working with them, not against them. The first principle is love.

Compassion in leadership must extend beyond the children to how colleagues are treated. Loving and leading means showing practical compassion when it is most needed. I often hear of teachers who have had to miss their own children's key moments at school (first day, school productions, etc.) because the head teacher won't let them have an hour or two off. Or teachers who are not allowed to go to a funeral because the school policy says it must be a certain type of relative. Or those who are pressured to come in when they are ill. Or teachers who could only dream of the flexibility of attending a wedding abroad or a 50th birthday lunch. If you love and trust your staff, then compassion demands your flexibility as a leader to look out for their well-being. That means giving them time off when they need it, allowing leave when necessary and being sensitive to personal circumstances.

At Parklands, there is an acceptance that we will look after each other whenever necessary. You might say there is an eagerness to do so. We all rely on each other so much that we don't want to see anyone struggling. We will step in to support a colleague, cover lessons when needed and take personal circumstances into account. Recognising that we all have lives beyond the school gates makes people feel trusted and builds loyalty. We are a team, not in competition with each other.

We hold training events towards the end of each summer holiday, and if colleagues attend they are given a day off in lieu to use when they need it. Yes, you read that correctly – a flexible day in lieu. In fact, everyone starts off with one day to use when required. Even if staff don't come to the team-building day in the summer holidays, they still get one day. Do the team-building and they already have two days in the bag before term starts. If staff volunteer for the week-long residential, they get another two days in lieu. An additional day is available for colleagues who help out on any of the other residential trips.

It is also possible to save up these days over two or three years. Staff then have some flexibility to react to events in their personal lives, plan for special events or simply to take a shopping day before Christmas. I don't want colleagues feeling like they have to lie to me or to anyone else to find their work–life balance. Nobody should have to fake an illness to go to a friend's wedding or funeral. Where is the dignity in that? So, we give our staff time. In truth, they earn time and are in control of how to use it.

Of course, the immediate assumption is that some people will try to take advantage of an approach that at first sight might appear overgenerous. Nobody takes advantage. In fact, colleagues pay back any time they take off for personal reasons over and over again. It used to be that all teachers were treated in this way. They would never complain about turning up after hours or even at the weekend. The profession ran on strong good-will. Head teachers had discretion and it was generally felt that if you looked after people they would reciprocate. Unfortunately, trust has been eroded across the system. The eagerness to impose corporate structures was a foreseeable error. Performance-related pay killed goodwill, stone dead.

Creating the conditions by which we could allow staff to have flexible lieu days to meet personal commitments needed some strategic and financial planning. We began looking at the accounts to see what could be rejigged to make it happen. We didn't have to look very hard. I was shocked to discover that food boxes were being delivered on a regular basis. Wine hampers and fresh food gifts would suddenly appear at my door. There were boxes of chocolates all over the office and cakes appearing from nowhere. I did wonder where they were coming from (okay, after I had munched through a few cream slices and snuck a few more to hungry children). I soon realised that they were being sent from supply teaching agencies as 'corporate gifts' – that is, edible bribes. I then discovered that these agencies were gently grazing off the school budget while trying to fatten up the head teacher. In 2013–2014, the year before I started, the school spent a staggering £185,000 on supply teacher costs.

It was an easy decision to employ two non-class-based teachers using some of that £185,000. Supply agencies were charging the school £250 per day but they were only paying the teachers £90. That didn't sit right with me – it felt like profiteering – so I banned them from the school. They didn't like it, but we have a responsibility to look after the money we get from government. Companies deserve to make a margin but this was going too far. The hampers, chocolate boxes and food platters stopped, which made my stomach a little sad but our values a little stronger.

Having non-class-based teachers means that we can cover class teachers whenever we need to, even when the request is at the last minute. Our cover teachers know the children, they are soaked in the school culture and they are a full part of the team. When colleagues are away the transition to a cover teacher is seamless. There is no churn of adults, which means that the children are not having to constantly meet new teachers who don't know the Parklands way. The effect of such stable staffing on behaviour and learning is obvious to anyone walks the corridors on a day when a staff member is away. You would never know who was out. Classes sustain their impeccable standards.

In addition, time is saved. When people are forced to fake an illness, one day doesn't seem convincing, so they often take off two days. Return after a single day off and colleagues are trying not to raise an eyebrow. Return after two days and people tend to be more sympathetic. By allowing everyone to be honest, the extra days of staff absence that happen just for effect disappear. This is a significant amount of time saved across the year. For example, I have got a Canadian member of staff. If her mum has flown in for a visit, I don't want her to ring up and say, '[Cough] I'm not coming in today.' I can say, 'Oh, you've got three days. Take your three days in lieu. We've got staff to cover you.' Not only are we saving money compared to previous years, but absence for sickness has also reduced dramatically.

When my housemate (who wasn't a teacher) got married, he set the date for a Friday. At the time, I had one of those head teachers who, if I had asked to go to a wedding, it could have gone either way with her. If she was in a good mood, she might have said yes. If she was in a bad mood, it would have been no. But I had to go to the wedding. I had house-shared with my friend for four years. We were good mates. He had even been good enough to hold his stag do during half term, which cost everyone else more money. Because I couldn't risk it, I had to take a sick day, and then to make it more realistic I had to make it a two-day sick day. I am sure many teachers have experienced similar conflicts.

As a parent, I was desperate to see my lovely daughter Daisy when she was asked to play the angel in the Christmas production of *Whoops-a-Daisy Angel*. She was only 4 and I was so proud she had got the main part. The problem is that most schools just do a morning and afternoon performance. They don't do an evening show for the little ones. This time I went to my head teacher and asked, 'Please can I go and see my daughter? She's in *Whoops-a-Daisy Angel*.' She replied, 'Who's going to teach your class? Of course you can't go.' I never got to see her in that role, and these chances don't come round a second time. We do things differently at Parklands. Nobody ever has to have that conversation.

I said to my staff at the very start: 'If anybody has got a Christmas concert, if anyone has got a sports day, if anyone is going to see their child play a match, it's not a lieu day. You just go.' It is all based on trust. If your child is performing in a concert, you will go and watch them.

Building a New Team from a Broken One

In my first few days as a head teacher, I noticed that the teachers were like rabbits caught in the headlights whenever they saw me. They thought I was there to give them a roasting and a telling-off. They had learned from bitter experience that head teachers were to be avoided at all costs.

I was actually there to give them support, but nobody was persuaded of that. Staff would panic and the blood would drain from their cheeks when I turned the corner. It was very strange, but they had been through the wringer in the previous few years. I understood why. My challenge was to get the team to work together, not through fear but collaboration. I had to do something different.

There was a training day coming up and I said to all the staff, 'Be outside the school at 9am. Put some trainers on because we're going on a team-building day.' But I didn't tell them where they were going. It was a Dyson Mystery Trip.

At 9am, all the staff – the teachers, teaching assistants, caretakers, everyone – piled onto two buses and we went to Hazlewood Castle to do some classic team-building tasks: orienteering, clay pigeon shooting and archery. We spent two hours working together in teams on a gloriously sunny day. Then we got back onto the coaches. Everyone was asking if we could carry on team building for the rest of the day. I told them we were only halfway through the adventure. We travelled on to York where I had hired a boat.

Colleagues thought we would be focusing on English and maths during the afternoon, but I wanted to come at things from a different angle. The staff had been working extra hours and doing endless twilight training sessions, but it had had little impact. It was time to stop going round in ever-decreasing circles. The teaching staff were tired and deserved to be spoilt. They were overwhelmed and under-trusted.

As we drifted slowly down the river on the boat, people began to relax and open up. It felt special. It felt like a new beginning. Someone mentioned that we should have got some sandwiches because they were starting to feel hungry. What they didn't know was that the final part of the day was a meal at a riverside pub where I had pre-ordered a carvery for everyone. Now, obviously, I couldn't buy the staff drinks with school money, but lunch was part of the training day. I made sure that nobody had to pay. At one point, I was talking to a few of the teaching assistants and they were in tears. I thought to myself, don't you like this? They said they had been at the school for many years and never once had they been treated so well.

It was a great day and the best way to pull people together. I think it made the impact I wanted. The first seeds of a new approach were sown. A strategy based on love, compassion and trust.

Professional Development

As a teacher, I used to dislike going on day-long maths courses when three quarters of the content wasn't relevant to me. It is quite strange that for many teachers this is their experience of CPD. When all you provide for staff is blanket, generic training you are throwing a big net that doesn't catch many fish. A lot of teachers' precious time can be wasted with poorly planned CPD. Paying people to sit and listen to things that have no relevance to their role whatsoever is madness.

We needed to upgrade the CPD offer at Parklands. Our challenge was to create a sharper, more focused and personalised professional development offer for each member of staff that would complement their role. If we could convert squandered time into productive training, our theory was that people might actually develop professionally. When I first came to Parklands, staying awake during a twilight session was a mark of success. My expectations for professional learning were way beyond that.

As a school, we were proactive on this from the start. We didn't want to waste any time at all. Everyone had experienced the inefficiencies of endless twilight training sessions. We made sure that all training was bespoke from the outset. It needed to be useful and practical. We brought in experts to deliver tailored CPD training rather than one-size-fits-all instruction. We needed to work smarter. Knowing your providers is vital. It is best to engage firms that have been strongly recommended by schools in similar circumstances.

If we needed some training in phonics, for example, there was no point in my Year 6 teacher doing it. I know it might have been nice for everyone to hear about what was going on in phonics, but that wouldn't be relevant to teachers of older children. Instead, we brought in someone who could deliver role-specific training. Better training, more targeted, means less time wasted.

We wanted to improve our approach to working with children who are higher ability in maths, specifically in Years 5 and 6. I asked Karen Knapper, a maths school improvement consultant from Leeds City Council, to deliver bespoke training with a focus on stretch and challenge for these children. She delivered two hours with one teacher, two hours with another teacher and two hours with another. Individuals got the training that would have the highest impact.

If our motivation for the training is special educational needs, we might want a short whole-school session to start the day but then we will branch off into smaller groups. We might need some colleagues to have training on autism, some on dyslexia and others to examine the impact of trauma on learning. It is about knowing your staff, understanding their needs and making sure communication is good.

Alternatively, a trainer may deliver material tailored to teaching assistants. This might involve an hour with all the teaching assistants, followed by small groups or one-to-one training focused on their children's priorities. In this way, the discussion stays rich and relevant. Nothing needs to be translated from a big folder marked 'CPD' or distilled down from a 'big ideas' presentation.

CPD that feels like it is for someone else is frustrating for busy professionals. Rather than using performance management as a stick with which to beat people, we jointly identify the training that individuals want and need. We then support them to do just that. We have six 90-minute sessions booked in for next year. Each of those training sessions might have eight different CPD opportunities going on at the same time.

Our staff are very good at sharing too. We make sure there is time allocated to this. At every other staff meeting, someone different will report back on an external course they have attended. This might be a paid course or perhaps a free TeachMeet or BrewEd. They are given time to prepare the presentation and focus on explaining the CPD they have done and examining how it might influence their role. We don't expect a cascade of information, although some key learning points from one colleague can spark ideas in others.

Bespoke CPD has been so successful and so well received that we have doubled our budget on it. With the explosion of online training opportunities that budget can now go a great deal further. We blend live sessions with virtual seminars, and instead of the old paper packs (handed out and then discarded), colleagues can secure their understanding by exploring more online. We build long-term relationships with trainers who understand the Parklands culture and approach. The needs of our staff and children drive the CPD offer. We are not interested in the latest fad unless it is a perfect fit for our school. We have learned to filter out the voices that don't work for us.

At Parklands, we have the time and flexibility for teachers and support professionals to work interchangeably with one another. The coaching and support comes from the team. We have got a teacher who is best at maths, a teacher who is best at reading, at writing, at topic work, at science, at art, at PE. Knowing those strengths, and making sure the staff know their strengths too, is what makes it work.

People come from far and wide to visit Parklands and find out more about what we do. The increasing number of visitors was partly the prompt to write this book. We invite people to spend the morning with us, to look in on the teaching and learning, to experience an assembly and a times table face-off, and to talk to our children about their school lives. The school is no longer a backwater through which nobody travels. It is now a five-star destination, and people from all over the UK and further afield want to come and learn from us.

Working in a school that is a beacon of good practice means that our staff are not just respected by the children and families close to them, they are also admired from far away. There is a real sense of pride in that.

Grandpa

Growing up, we never had massive Christmas presents like my children receive now. But one thing we did have was a lot of love. We were a very close family. My mum and dad were only children, so we didn't have cousins or aunties or uncles, but we did have my mum's mum and dad. They were a massive part of my life. My grandpa was a butcher for 45 years with a shop opposite Sheffield Wednesday's football stadium. He was an inspiration, and he always made sure we had food on the table. We got to enjoy the delights of tripe (some of you will know that taste now) and kidneys (still one of my favourites). We always had a beautiful meal, no matter what.

My grandpa was a true hard worker. Dedicated and reliable. When his boss Mr Webb died, he left the butcher's shop to my grandpa in his will as a thank you for being such a loyal and committed worker. That sort of patronage is unheard of now. I spoke about this at my grandpa's funeral. Grandpa was like a dad to me. In the end, he owned the butcher's shop for 30 years. He loved it. My brother did too. He worked there every Saturday from 12 years old all the way up to 18. Unfortunately, I wasn't allowed to as I was too lively. I would play knock and run on the nearby houses, and then I would be brought into the shop in disgrace (regularly), so I was banned from the shop.

Grandpa retired at 70 at a time when smaller shops were being swallowed up by supermarkets. The butcher's shop used to stand in a row along with a greengrocer, florist and newsagent. It was a typical shopping parade of the type that served a local community, where you would pop into one shop and then into another. The arrival of supermarkets and everyone driving to buy their weekly shop meant that the butchers closed and became a fancy-dress shop. It broke my heart. But grandpa got out at the right time – just before the big stores took all of his business.

His love, generosity and sense of community are never forgotten. He put food in our bellies even when times were tough. His compassion drives my decision-making every day.

Last Christmas ...

At Christmas 2020, we were given £12,000 from an anonymous source. It was a surprise gift and was in response to the government's reluctance to fund free school meals for children over the holidays. With such a generous donation, we really wanted to get the best deal for the school and the community. I rang up Aldi and asked if I could order £12,000 worth of food vouchers, so we could feed all the kids over Christmas. I offered them £10,000 for the vouchers. They were cautious at first but with a little persuasion they agreed. I then got my secretary to order another £2,000 of vouchers, so we ended up with £14,000 in vouchers. Every child, teacher, cleaner, lunch supervisor, support professional, teaching assistant and member of office staff received a £40 Aldi voucher for Christmas as a thank you. They were so appreciative because they weren't expecting it.

Treating staff well means they don't move on so quickly. Our community needs stability in their school, so they love people who stick around. The children need stability most of all. A constant churn of adults at school can be particularly difficult for children who have disrupted home lives.

When staff mobility is at 50% or 60% each year, everyone is just getting used to new people and then they move on. When you have got a settled team, everyone feels that it is worth investing in relationships. We have transformed staff retention at Parklands and turnover is no longer an issue. We have lost four staff in seven years, three of whom left because of a promotion.

It seems that when you love your staff hard enough they become a work family. It is easy to leave a job, but it is hard to leave a family, even for the day. There were 623 sick days in the year before I started as head teacher at Parklands. This figure is now down to less than one day's absence per member of staff.

At Parklands we like to grow our own staff, identify potential early and help individuals to achieve beyond their own ambition. It is one of the key strengths of our school. A stable staff who have grown up and progressed soaked in the culture of Parklands are like gold dust. If we don't develop them, they either get stale or they leave for lack of opportunity. Of course, sometimes people need to move on to find wider opportunities. We see that as successful development. But it is still hard to leave when you are loved.

When I work as a national leader of education, I take our maths lead, English lead or special educational needs coordinator with me for their own CPD. This really helps them to learn from and influence schools that need support. When we have visitors to our school, staff members take key roles in leading the day. They are interacting with people from a huge range of context and cultures, and they grow in confidence each time.

Staff well-being is about the big stuff as well as the small considerations. Our staff are incredible and keen to learn more. It is vital that we feed their ambition, alongside feeding them cake!

Parklands Fundamentals

- Love the adults you have got and find common ground with all of them. Celebrate the fact that every person has their strengths.

- Give colleagues the flexibility to manage personal priorities. Generosity breeds loyalty.

- Provide a properly tailored CPD offer where the staff choose their developmental paths instead of being told what to learn.

- If your families need feeding then that must be the priority, whether that is term time or holiday time.

- Kindness and generosity drive goodwill and take on their own momentum.

What a great set of pupils, they were so full of confidence and enthusiasm. They gave it 100%. The staff were so happy as well.

Jeff Rich, former drummer of Status Quo

Chapter 6
Achievement

Chapter 6
Achievement

Building a school on love means little if the children aren't learning and achieving. To make Parklands into a high-achieving school, we had work to do. My plan was simple: give them a dream, believe in them and chase it hard.

I had always prided myself on teaching times tables as a class teacher. I knew the pleasure the children had in becoming confident so quickly and the pride they took in getting faster and faster. I wanted everyone to taste that kind of success, and so I set about challenging classes on their times tables. It became my thing, and it was the first step in addressing the achievement gap across the school. Bridging that gap is partly about knowledge, but it is also about experiencing success.

I would pop into classes on a Monday and Tuesday and ask the children to play times table tennis with me. I would say '4', and they would respond with '8', '12' or '16'. It is a very traditional teaching method, but I put a spin on it. On Wednesday I would ask for 'four 8s' or 'four 6s'. They enjoyed the variety and the competition. It took me two terms to get all the kids to learn all their times tables. I did it by relentlessly visiting classrooms and making it important. Later on, the Times Tables Rock Stars platform added a new dimension as it allowed the children to practise their tables at home. It produced one of the biggest impacts the school has seen: low investment for maximum results.

Once they knew their tables, I made it harder by asking for the answer to the times table to be subtracted from 100. Times tables made harder? The children loved it! They switched on to it immediately. Don't let anyone tell you that children don't want to learn. They are hungry for it. It was like they had been waiting to fly.

As a new head teacher building a new culture, I had the perfect excuse for short bursts of Dyson in the middle of classes. The kids were responding to it too. Even within that first week, when you walked into a room, you didn't have to duck any more. Now, the kids would sit up, knowing that I would ask them questions. My mentor and school improvement adviser said that I should stop doing this because it disrupted the learning. It was a fair observation, but I felt the disruption was worth it. I ignored their advice and stuck to my guns.

As soon as the children's motivation is sparked, behaviour starts improving and teachers' working lives become so much easier. They don't have to police the pupils any more. Previously they were crowd-managing rather than inspiring.

One term in, and there were still teachers waiting for me to enter lessons and expecting some kind of judgement. It was always going to take time. Planning lessons alongside staff enabled more trust to build between us. We would plan together and then I would deliver the lesson with them. On the following day, I would watch them deliver a lesson alone and then provide feedback. It would be more of a coaching conversation rather than an inspector's tick-list. I developed a regular routine so that once a day I was teaching a lesson or feeding back to a colleague. The teaching team had a month of my time spaced throughout that first year. Eight years on, and we see our brilliant teachers coaching each other. You just need to get the ethos right.

I have learned that when trying to raise achievement you can't rush anything. You have to take your time to embed changes. When I first arrived at Parklands it felt like everything needed changing. It would have been easy to start lots of initiatives all at once and then watch all of them struggle to take off. I had the experience of being a deputy, so I knew that planning change over time is critical. We desperately wanted to raise achievement and show the children and the community that they were as full of potential as any child, but we had to take things one step at a time. For example, when we started developing our consistent approach to teaching writing, we would share ideas and look at what worked and didn't work. We had 12 weeks of trial and error to research and test approaches before committing to a strategy.

To make things easy for staff, I decided early on that I would devise a whole-school timetable. Previously, each teacher had decided on their own timetable. But I didn't want some kids doing reading while others were doing phonics or times tables. My main priority was to make room in the timetable for everyone to do Early Bird Maths at the same time every day. From my previous experience, I knew the impact that daily maths, done first thing in the morning, can have on children. I was prescriptive but that was important.

There is now a rhythm to the school day at Parklands which is shared by all. When the children pour out into the yard, they are all talking about the last lesson and they are all talking about the same subject. Similarly, teachers dipping into one another's classrooms can see how far other year groups have come and observe how they are being taught. It is peak collaboration and works beautifully. It is so much easier to monitor progression between years, to focus on pedagogy and to have a consistent approach when the whole school is following the same timetable.

We also agreed as a team that we wouldn't check lesson plans but we would look at the children's books. Checking planning is a lot of work for small gains. If teachers are always trying to perfect their planning for someone else's benefit, they may be wasting time that could be spent on an inspirational lesson for the children.

Inspection Isn't Always a Dirty Word

A very significant event occurred after my first year in post, which was one of the biggest turning points for our school. We had a subject inspection in maths; the inspector was Adrian Guy. We knew it would be a big test. Even though it was a subject inspection, if he had seen our behaviour six months earlier, then we would have been in big trouble.

We showed Adrian our best Year 2 maths whizz-kid, who was an incredible mental mathematician and had pages of correct work on multiplication in his book. We were told it was not impressive at all. We thought that was outrageous, but Adrian pointed out that we needed breadth rather than depth in one area. His challenge was: 'If a pupil can do four long multiplication questions correctly, why do you need to see six sides?' He was right. Adrian helped us to write our maths action plan for the next year. We soaked up every word he fed back to us. There were no excuses from us. We wanted to use his knowledge and expertise to take us further, faster. It was outstanding professional development for us all.

I was honest with Adrian about behaviour. He told me that we were nowhere near a good school, but we were heading in the right direction. He thought we were somewhere between inadequate and requires improvement. Because of our honesty and the plans we had in place, he did not recommend a section 8 inspection, but he did warn us of a future inspection. We didn't challenge it; we just accepted it. His advice was really significant because it helped us to formulate our future maths plans and put us on the front foot in terms of fluency and reasoning in maths. It also demonstrated that our behaviour work to date had been effective.

We now had an excellent plan with which to move forward. There are many criticisms of inspection regimes, but when you find a great inspector who is willing to help the school make progress, it is like a breath of fresh air.

One of the problems I find when I am working as a national leader of education is that schools are often trying to change everything all at once. They are attempting to revolutionise reading, writing and maths simultaneously. For example, I visited a school two years ago that was doing a reading twilight followed by maths and writing twilights. It is so much better to go slowly and take small steps, to trial things first, to assess what went well and what didn't. Initiative overload is a very real problem in school improvement. One thing at a time is my mantra at Parklands; it is even on the school improvement plan.

Inspector Love

I have been waiting for this phone call for three years; every day I have got up and thought, it will be today that it rings. I am a bit strange in that I have always adored Ofsted inspections. I think it is fantastic CPD. It is great to be able to reflect as a teacher, as a deputy head, as a senior leader and now as a head teacher. The focus can never be on preparing for Ofsted. It is more important to use your energy to know your school and know where you want to go.

We knew the answers to these questions, so in 2017 we were so ready for a new inspection to take us from the inadequate grade that the local authority had bestowed on us.

I was in a Year 2 classroom flying drones around when suddenly all of the walkie-talkies sparked into life: 'Does anyone know where Chris is?' 'Chris to the office.' I sauntered back to my office only to be met in the corridor by three office staff in an agitated state: 'Ofsted is on the phone.'

I got the tingles. This was it. I walked very quickly to my room (there is no running in the school) and picked up the phone with a 'Yabba-Dabba-Doo! I have been waiting for your call. I'm so excited – we can't wait to meet you all.'

Good morning Chris,

On behalf of myself and Darren, I just wanted to say a big thank you to you, your staff, your governors and your wonderful pupils.

Your hospitality was much appreciated, as was your open and receptive participation in the day.

We both really enjoyed our time with you. We often say our job is a privilege. It was certainly a privilege spending some time in your school.

Best wishes for the future,

Sue Eastwood
Her Majesty's Inspector, North West Region

Early Bird Maths and Same-Day Interventions

The moment the children come into school in the morning we have Early Bird Maths – and what an impact it has had. It runs from 8.50am to 9.10am every day. The children do set questions from the board, with the challenge of getting 20 answers correct. This is their warm-up. Some children may only get to 10; there is a broad range of ability. If we do 20 minutes a day, five days a week, that is 100 minutes a week. Multiply that by 36 weeks, which is the school year, that is 3,600 minutes. Divide that by 24 and it gives you 65 extra hours of maths just by coming into school on time every day. All of this is in addition to timetabled maths lessons.

From 9.10am to 9.20am, the teacher guides the children in maths strategies. (Sometimes it is a little more, sometimes a little less.) All the pupils then do a task from 9.20am until 9.35am from the White Rose Maths scheme (https://whiterosemaths.com). Finally, the teacher reads out the answers to the task and the children self-mark. They do this every day, including the last day before the Christmas break and the final day of the summer term in July.

At the end of Early Bird Maths, the children put their books in the coloured tray that best indicates how much they have understood. If they haven't got a clue what has happened they put their book in the red tray; to say 'Will you just check it for me?' they put their book in the yellow tray; or to say 'Yay, I'm all good' they put their book in the green tray. We have an assembly from 9.40am until 10am every day. While the children are in assembly, often led by me, the teacher will look at the books and identify those who require support and those who can move on to mastery work.

When the children come back from assembly, between 10am and 10.30am, is what we call 'same-day intervention', when the teacher works with the children who need the most help (rather than with a random group). The children then go back into class with specific learning tasks that have emerged from the teacher's marking. Meanwhile, the rest of the class are doing fluency work – embedding the knowledge and demonstrating that they have understood the new concept.

And so the learning progresses. It is never stagnant and never gets boring. This technique has produced outstanding results (see Tables 6.1 and 6.2). Why wait until the next day to see which children require support when we can be proactive and develop the children that day?

Table 6.1. End of Key Stage 2 progress measures, 2019–2021

Parklands Primary School	Reading 2019	Reading 2020	Reading 2021	Writing 2019	Writing 2020	Writing 2021	Maths 2019	Maths 2020	Maths 2021
Progress score	3.1	1.6	4.3	4.4	3.4	4.6	4.8	2.7	4.3
Lower confidence interval	1.3	-0.4	2.2	2.7	1.6	2.6	3.2	0.7	2.2
Upper confidence interval	5.0	3.6	6.5	6.1	5.4	6.7	6.4	4.7	6.4
Significance	Sig+	-	Sig+	Sig+	Sig+	Sig+	Sig+	Sig+	Sig+

Table 6.2. Progress in reading, writing and maths, 2018–2019 (latest data)

	Reading	Writing	Maths
School progress score	+3.54	+3.99	+8.47
Confidence interval	*+1.45 to +5.64*	*+2.01 to 5.96*	*+6.63 to 10.31*
Well above national average (about 10% of schools in England)	✓	✓	✓
Above national average (about 10% of schools in England)			
Average (about 60% of schools in England)			
Below national average (about 10% of schools in England)			
Well below national average (about 10% of schools in England)			
Number of pupils	34	36	36

Our progress figures over several years demonstrate the excellent progress that has historically been achieved at Parklands and which has been continued over the last two years despite the challenges of the COVID-19 pandemic. Since 2017, nearly all progress measures have been significantly above average, and many of them have been in the top 10.5% of schools nationally. The majority of our pupils are officially identified as *disadvantaged* and nearly all of our pupils live in very deprived areas. These whole-school figures demonstrate how we deliver transformative outcomes for our children despite all of the challenges they face, supporting them every step of the way from well-below-average on-entry attainment to well-above-average achievement by the end of Key Stage 2.[1]

Traditionally, interventions are delivered by teaching assistants. We wanted to flip this and get the teacher to do the same-day interventions. This frees up the teaching assistants to walk around the room with an answer sheet for the fluency work the other pupils are getting on with. Another advantage of same-day interventions is that, as the name suggests, all the work is marked on the same day, so there is no maths homework to take home. This has an instant impact on teachers' workload and well-being.

As Early Bird Maths learning starts at 8.50am, it has also had a positive effect on punctuality. If parents think the children are walking into a fairly loose registration period, there is little urgency. If the children know that the learning doesn't start on the dot, they dawdle. With Early Bird Maths, the slow parents are being dragged along the road by their children. Everyone wants to start on time.

Our pupils are sharp with numbers because they have been doing it every day for years. Laura Darley, my deputy head teacher, and Brooke Nolan, one of my assistant head teachers, were instrumental in making Early Bird Maths such a success and then assisting in rolling it out to other schools. White Rose Maths have also played a huge part in our mastery work.

---

1   Ian Stokes Education, *Beyond the School Gates*, p. 28.

TES Schools Awards

Beth Bennett, Brooke Nolan and I went down to London on behalf of the school for the TES Schools Awards in 2018. We had been nominated in two categories: Head Teacher of the Year and Maths School of the Year. We were excited. The school had come a long way in the previous three years and to get recognition for that would be a huge lift for the staff, children and community.

Walking into the ballroom at the Grosvenor House Hotel took my breath away. It was a world away from Parklands. It was fully decked out with twinkly lights, sparkling glasses and posh cutlery. We were surrounded by incredible teachers and leaders. It was an amazing evening, but the results didn't go our way.

I wasn't bothered about not winning Head Teacher of the Year. It would have been lovely, but I didn't have any sense of disappointment. But not winning Maths School of the Year hit me harder than I expected. It would have been the perfect recognition for the staff who had worked so hard and come so far. I wanted to return to Parklands with a trophy to share. Silly really.

Later that evening, Beth and Brooke found me wandering the streets of Kings Cross consumed with disappointment. They saved me from my misery and dragged me back to the hotel. In the clear light of day, for the school to be even considered for a national award was an achievement; to make the shortlist in two categories just a few years from being in chaos was unheard of. We still had a lot of which to be proud. After all, we had won the TES Collaboration Award in 2017. It might be that I am just a bit greedy!

Parklands Fundamentals

▣ Everyday maths means exceptional achievement instantly and over time.

▣ Times tables are more than just a game. They are a gateway to making maths fun and fractions/division a lot simpler.

▣ Bridging the achievement gap takes time, but it is definitely bridgeable.

▣ Inspectors are human too. Their feedback is really useful if you are open to it.

▣ Same-day interventions work for staff and children.

We can honestly say that every class we visited had an amazing buzz around maths. The resources were plentiful and the children really could explain the depth of their thinking. The times tables from Year 1 to Year 6 simply were breathtaking.

Caroline Hamilton, White Rose Maths, Trinity Academy

Chapter 7

Parents, Community and Family

Chapter 7

Parents, Community and Family

'This is your school, this is your community – come and share it with us. And, if you don't come, I'm going to badger you until you do!'

I had to build relationships with the parents at Parklands from day one. We were expecting 45 new children to arrive in reception. Most didn't show up on the first day. It spoke volumes. There were so many parents who didn't want to send their child to the school: 'Over my dead body is my child going to Parklands.' It was clear that there were baked-in problems.

I called each family to invite them in. I wanted to show them around the school and tell them about my ambitious vision for the future. I sold it that way – and it was a hard sell. The reputation of the school had not been good. I explained that I had only just started and that they needed to give me a chance. I had to beg for their support on occasion. They had been let down so many times before. I had to get those relationships going, and the best way, as always, was face to face.

When you get the parents onside, the kids are happy and the parents are too. It all comes down to communication. If parents have got a problem, I don't say, 'Right, come and see me a week on Thursday.' I have got an open-door policy. If there is a problem, parents want their voice to be heard now, not tomorrow. Nobody wants to see grievances popping up on social media, snowballing a tiny issue into a major crisis, especially as this is an estate school. So, my door is open. I will always be there to listen and solve problems while they are still small. Love doesn't need an appointment.

Having an open-door policy makes such a difference, but don't make the mistake of assuming that you have to react immediately. Picking up the phone in anger is never going to end well. Neither is making a decision after just one testimony. It is important to back your staff in public, even if you need to have a quiet word with them in private. Be slow to judge; those extra few minutes could save hours of work rebuilding trust (and backtracking) later on. Parents just want to be heard, so lend them your ears. Diverting the parent briefly onto other conversations can often take the sting out of their frustration. It reminds them that we are there to work with them, not against them. It reminds them that we are not the bad guys.

It was hard during COVID-19 with little face-to-face interaction with parents. We needed to make more of an effort to ensure that communication was good. And we are persistent. The parent who pretends to be on the phone every time they drop off their kids, we see you. The parents who ignore emails from the school, we notice. Our persistence with parents is our secret sauce. We don't give up. We will remind them of meetings before they happen. We will make that call at a time when we know they might answer. We are patient and relentless.

In 2017, two parents who had been against sending their children to Parklands told the Ofsted inspection team the story of their children's journey at the school. The inspector told me later, 'If you had heard what she said about the school, it would have brought tears to your eyes.' It is gratifying that some of these anxious parents are now on our governing body.

When the children decided to spend the £10,000 playground money on an assault course, we dug the foundations and then overnight someone stole all the timber. I knocked on the door of one of the leading figures in the community who lived nearby and observed that it was disappointing that the wood had been nicked. By the following morning, the timber had been returned. The family of the individual I approached wasn't involved, but they had called around and found someone who knew someone who knew someone else who was.

I thought it would be really difficult to get the commitment of parents, but they engaged with me straight away. Speaking to the community was key. Going onto the estate was key. There was no mention of the police being involved. There were no threats about what would happen if the wood wasn't returned. It was just an honest conversation that pulled at the heartstrings of the community. As the building materials were uninsured, it was going to be their children and grandchildren who would pay the price for the assault course not being built. The fact that all the timber was replaced showed how, in a short time, the community was getting on board. It was a very significant moment for the school. The news that I had actually visited the house of a well-known community figure and asked for help spread like wildfire.

Feeding and Well-being

Food is very important in areas of poverty. That sounds obvious, but few people can imagine growing up with empty cupboards. Or homes where adults don't eat so their children can. Or homes where nobody eats with any regularity. Or homes where addiction has taken hold. Often, they are proud parents who work their socks off but still can't balance the money every month, or they are parents who are going through hard times. We all need food. Whatever the choices or fortunes of the adults, every child has a right to eat.

You might not consider that schools should be responsible for addressing food poverty. You might be right, but we will not sit by and watch families go hungry. Politicians can make decisions about what the government will provide. While they are arguing, we are going to feed our families. We see the impact on children who are well fed in our classrooms every day. Food is fuel for learning, for emotional control and for well-being. Families know how much it matters too. Food binds the school to its community with every mouthful. Trust is built through giving. When the school gives so much and asks for nothing in return, it is no longer them and us. It is just us.

Children don't learn well on empty stomachs. Experts tell us that breakfast is the most important meal of the day, and that children who eat a good breakfast achieve higher grades in school than children who don't.

We want our pupils to thrive in school, so we hold a breakfast club every morning for everyone from 8am. Without it, some children might not eat until lunchtime, which could be 18 hours after they last ate.

We receive a life-changing amount of food during the year, so we can ensure that none of our children go hungry. Breakfast is not just toast and tea. We are grateful to Kraft Heinz, Nestlé, Kellogg's, New York Bakery Company, Tropicana Products and Scottish Porridge Oats for their generous and unwavering support, all courtesy of the brilliant Magic Breakfast (www.magicbreakfast.com). Our breakfast club is just a small part of what we do now, but it is so important.

During the first national lockdown, our response as a school was all about food. When we had to close the school on 23 March 2020, I promised the children that no one would go without on my watch. I went out into the playground and said that if anyone needed anything, we would be in school every day and we would help out. We worked hard and made sure that we balanced the doom and gloom of the pandemic with a serious amount of food. I had the happiest families of lockdown. Food hampers were going to the children's homes twice a week and included groceries from Yorkshire Tea, Costa Coffee, McCain Foods and Whitby Seafoods. At Parklands, lockdown has not led to more food deprivation.

Bringing Food to the Table

Adam Smith, who is the founder of the Real Junk Food Project (https:// trjfp.com), collects food from supermarkets that is close to its sell-by date and is about to go to landfill. He has set up his own cafes where they recycle food and sell meals for just £2. I went to a head teacher's forum where Adam was speaking and he came across as a real community builder, a real person for the people.

There are millions of tons of food going to waste every day. Adam can bring it into schools for £400 a year, which covers the cost of the delivery van (the Real Junk Food Project is a non-profit making organisation).

We get a delivery twice a week from Adam and his team. The food is totally free to our families. They just bring the carrier bags and there is always enough to go around.

About 40–45 vulnerable families take priority and get to come in and fill their bags at 2.15pm. We let the children choose the food, with a little help: 'Right, what do you want? Get some apples. Look at all those oranges and all those pears – get them in as well. Look, bananas, and bread too. Banana sandwiches for your tea!' At 3.15pm, when the parents come to collect the children, it is open for everyone, so they all pop in and get what they need.

Many people don't want to eat food that has reached its expiration date, especially if they are from the leafy suburbs: 'Oh, we're not having that.' Whereas my parents were absolutely loving having cereals, flour and biscuits that were close to the sell-by date but still totally edible.

It is so important that our children learn with food in their bellies. We do everything possible to make sure that happens.

Two Quid

When I was 10, I 'signed' for Intake Juniors – my first ever football team. I couldn't have been happier. I got to play with my mates at a strong competitive level. I was a football addict: I lived for football; I would have died for football. I would be up at 4am getting ready to play at the weekend. As soon as it was light, I would be outside kicking a ball, waking up the entire house, the neighbours and the neighbours' dog!

I didn't have a dad who could take me to football matches. I didn't go with my grandpa, even though his butchers shop was opposite Hillsborough Stadium (I am a Sheffield United fan, by the way), as he was working all day on a Saturday. Playing the game and playing for a good team meant everything to me.

I clearly remember one day when my mum sat me down and said, 'Chris, you can't go any more.' We couldn't afford the weekly £2 training fee. It broke my heart. My world fell apart a little. £2 a week doesn't sound like much, does it? But if you don't have it, you don't have it.

It is that moment more than any other that drives me. When I look back, it makes me want to give as much as I can to the children whose mums can't afford £2 a week. I don't want any other kids to be £2 short, ever.

The Night Before Christmas

It was 4 December 2014 and I was doing my normal walk around the school. As I did so, I got the Christmas tingles and started to get excited about the upcoming celebrations, the family getting together and of course, Santa. I decided to ask the children about Father Christmas. I found out that, sadly, only a small percentage of our children had ever been to a Santa's Grotto. The grottos are all in town and you need a car and money to get there. The cost is prohibitive. Mulling over some of the conversations I'd had with the children really made me think. I would be sitting down on Christmas Day and enjoying lots of food, drink, presents and excess. Many of these kids were not going to have a Christmastime like that. We needed to do something.

Our starting point was that every kid has a right to see Santa. I wanted Parklands children to have a festive experience like the one my own kids have. I called in my senior staff to say that I wanted to open the school on Christmas Day and lay on a simple Christmas lunch and a chocolate selection box for the kids. No one was keen to abandon their Christmas Day at such a late stage of planning, so we settled on Christmas Eve instead. We dragged in the early career teachers to help out and an idea was born. I set out my ambition and wrote to some local businesses. Our initial aim was to get 300 £1 selection boxes which we would wrap up, so when we opened the school on Christmas Eve every child would have a present. We haven't looked back.

Fortunately, and this is a little known fact, Santa resides in Canada in the off months. He is related to one of my Canadian teachers and flies over a little early because it is easier to deliver to Europe if he stops off at Parklands. Yes, Father Christmas comes to Parklands first!

I called a contact from Business in the Community, Mike Harvey, who I had worked with previously with business volunteers, and he was straight on it. He said, 'We'll get you 200 presents from Yorkshire Bank, Halifax, TD Direct Investing and other companies.' I couldn't believe it when the presents started arriving. It seemed that people wanted to go above and beyond for the children. It was astounding.

Businesses really went to town and were donating presents left, right and centre. In that first year, we managed to give out over 300 presents. Just seeing the look on the children's faces when they received their gift was – and still is – incredible. I know it is difficult to imagine for some, but there are some homes with no presents under the tree and others with no tree at all. For some children, the Christmas period means drunken relatives, domestic violence, neglect and no hot dinners.

We also provided 300 Christmas lunches for the children and their families to help create a feeling of community spirit and to show that we care. After all, everyone deserves to pull a cracker, try a sprout and enjoy a delicious meal. Without food donations, some children worry about eating on Christmas Day because 'all the takeaways are closed'. Imagine. When you work in an area of deprivation, the deprivation doesn't take a holiday. This is why Christmas Eve at Parklands is so important.

Unilever called up on the last day before we finished for the autumn term and asked, 'We have just seen what you are doing on Christmas Eve. Can we get involved?' I said, 'Sorry, but the school is closed. I think it might be too late – we have all the presents we need.' Instead, they brought in a snow machine and a team of reindeers, which were waiting outside the school with Santa's sleigh when the children arrived. What an amazing Christmas upgrade!

The Christmas Extravaganza

The Christmas Extravaganza is not just about Parklands, it is about the community in Seacroft. We open it up to everyone. On Christmas Eve 2020, we managed to serve 798 lunches and give away 798 presents. This is great because grandparents, older siblings, friends from other schools, aunts and uncles all come to the event. It really sets us up for Christmas. When I am tucking into my plate of turkey on Christmas Day, I can sit back and think: yesterday we gave time to make other people's Christmas special. It is arguably the best thing we do at the school and the best gift we could give.

Christmas Eve at Parklands needs some serious planning with so many people regularly attending. We now have to find 800 presents every year. It would still be okay to give everyone a selection box, but many businesses want to give more. With this luxury, we can try to make sure the children get a gift that is right for their age and interests. The thought might count, but if you are 7 years old and this is your only present, it matters. Some companies wrap the presents before delivering them, in which case, we need to ask them to split their donation in four ways: under 5s, under 7s, under 11s and over 11s. Of course, most companies don't wrap them, so I get in a crack team of parents to wrap hundreds of gifts in the weeks before Christmas.

With many of our parents out of work, 'wrapping season' can provide much-needed support and even work experience. Parents come into a work environment with a regular routine, tea, coffee and a school lunch, great conversations and a lot of social interaction (and laughter). The wrapping team get a feel for the rhythm and routine of work. As a reward, the helpers get first dibs on the presents. We let our crack team pick the present their child would like, wrap it, write their name on it and put it in Santa's bag. Then, when their child goes to see Santa, he already has the right present for them. We get some amazing donations too – scooters, bikes and gifts worth £40–50.

We have a room at school which is full of presents that haven't yet been gifted. We ended up with 1,200 the year before last, so we have always got hundreds in reserve. Some we donate to the local hospice, to the homeless or to children who are in temporary accommodation, but we never want to run out so we try to keep a stockpile. As we all know from *Joseph and the Amazing Technicolor Dreamcoat*, seven years of plenty might be followed by seven years of famine. It is important to have a stock for those black swan events, like COVID-19, when businesses may be struggling to keep themselves afloat and are unable to give as much.

The only people paid to attend the Christmas Extravaganza are the kitchen staff, which has to come out of the school budget. I mentioned this to a local property development business, Rushbond, and they immediately said they would give us £2,000 every year to pay the kitchen staff.

The Christmas Extravaganza isn't just about saying hello to Santa, grabbing a gift and leaving. It is a full Christmas experience for families with four different activities. We issue a ticket to everyone on arrival. The first 50 go to the Santa queue, the next 50 head for the bouncy castle, the next 50 go to the unicorns (life-size moving unicorns that interact with the children!) and the next 50 go straight to lunch. Then we all rotate.

For our parents, it has become a significant Christmas outing. It is a special four-hour activity at a time and place that is convenient to them. It is absolutely lovely to see. The happiness, smiles and gratitude that pour out is true community.

There is nothing better than walking through the school grounds on Christmas Eve with fake snow lying on the path. You might even come across 10-year-old lads, hard as nails, pointing at the reindeers and saying, 'Huh, look at them donkeys with sticks on their heads!' Every year, I have to persuade someone that they are actually reindeers. Lots of our children don't know reindeers are real because they have never seen them before.

We ran the initial Christmas Extravaganza at the end of my first term at Parklands. It was incredible how the community were already coming onside: 'We've never seen anything like this. We've never had anything like this. What a beautiful experience it is for our kids to come to this school!'

One Christmas, questions were raised over pupils who didn't attend our school being in the food queue. Some people wanted to send them away. I said that Santa doesn't send anyone away, so we gave them their lunch and a present too. We don't exclude people at Parklands. Christmas is about love. It is wonderfully aligned with our values.

In 2019, *The Guardian* got wind of what Parklands and other schools were doing and ran a fantastic double-page colour spread, including me wearing a Christmas tree print suit![1] Suddenly, the Christmas Extravaganza was getting national media attention. On the morning the article came out, my school business manager called me at 8.55am in a state of excitement. She said the phone was ringing off the hook with donations. At 9.30am, Sky News presenter Sarah-Jane Mee called: 'Can you come on live at 3.45pm and talk to us about it?' They made it 'interview of the week' and repeated it every hour over the weekend. Parklands had gone viral!

At first glance, this might look like me trying to get on the telly or see my picture in the paper. I can't tell you that I don't enjoy it, but these opportunities for nation-wide coverage have a direct impact on the pupils. They generate income which all goes to benefit the children – pure and simple.

When I returned to school having been on Sky News on Christmas Eve, we discovered that over £19,000 had been donated to the school by businesses and anonymous individuals. Every time we hit the headlines, we have the same response from kind-hearted people. The money paid for the children's residential trip the following year. People love to be charitable when they see where the money is going and when they can see a direct impact.

We weren't able to do a live Christmas Extravaganza in 2020 because of COVID-19, so we launched the Twelve Days of Christmas instead. In the run-up to Christmas, we asked different businesses to donate something – for example, chocolates, Christmas puddings and all those little festive things many of us take for granted. Some 340 luxury hampers were also sent home to all the children courtesy of Give a Gift in Leeds (https://giveagift.org.uk). The businesses that donate to Parklands tend to come back every year. They become our friends and supporters

---

1   Liz Lightfoot, 'Many of Our Children Don't Get Presents': Schools Open Over Christmas for Families with Nothing, *The Guardian* (17 December 2019). Available at: https://www.theguardian. com/education/2019/dec/17/children-dont-get-presents-schools-open-over-christmas.

through thick and thin. Their generosity, even during a pandemic, has been inspirational.

Time for a small confession. To my shame, during all of the work on the Christmas Extravaganza I have had to tell one lie. It is a Christmas fib, but a very necessary one, and I need to confess it here. When we first announced the Christmas lunches, and told everyone we would be having turkey, roast potatoes, Yorkshire puddings and all the trimmings, there were murmurings. The children were refusing to eat turkey because they 'don't like turkey' and were reluctant to take the risk. We soon realised that we were going to be left with a lot of turkey, so I swiftly made it known that there had been a mistake and that chicken had been delivered instead of turkey. They wolfed it down. So, at Parklands, 'turkey' is always pronounced 'chicken'.

How to Start Your Own Christmas Eve Extravaganza

- A Christmas Extravaganza takes time to build, so start small and make it manageable – perhaps a lunch and grotto to start with. It is like a snowball. When you are making a snowman, it starts with a little snowball and then builds its own momentum. It has taken us eight years to get where we are now.

- A small present for each child is a key aim. The school may be able to put up the initial seed money and buy just one gift for everyone. Contributors from business then see what is already happening which makes it easy for them to commit. They are joining a party, not having to make one on their own.

- Look to your local business contacts – everyone has got a Sainsbury's, Tesco, Asda or Aldi close by. They are the people with whom to build positive relationships. Most large national and multinational companies now have 'community champions' who are actively seeking to promote their business through local communities. What better way to promote yourselves than at Christmastime when it is all about giving?

> Don't just do a blanket email and copy in the big four supermarkets. Try to find out the name of the community champion, make contact with them and starting building a relationship. Get to the right person and then make it feel personal.

Establishing new ways of collaborating with parents evolved gradually at Parklands. It is no good organising a cheese and wine evening when everyone wants bingo. We always want to make sure that we meet parents on their own terms. The parents see us bending over backwards for them. We give them things that others don't. We provide opportunities that others won't. Fast forward to the present, and in reception we have double the applicants for places. We also have an extensive waiting list in every year group. The demand for places at Parklands is so high that we are constantly looking at how to grow.

Everyone knows that everything my own children get, the children at Parklands get too. This was demonstrated very clearly to parents when they realised that my own daughter would be attending the school. There is no clearer message to the community. The impact it has had cannot be underestimated. As well as being an obvious confidence-builder for community relations, Parklands provided a fabulous education for my daughter and is the best thing I ever did for my own well-being. Although I was working long hours, I could spend 45 minutes on the drive to and from work with my daughter. She became my best friend. I was really sad when she left Year 6 because all the time we had spent together was extremely valuable. It was a real bonus to have four years of travelling together.

Although a good deal of the relationship between school and home is informal, all of our parents sign a home–school contract in which expectations are made clear. We want to make sure they understand what we expect from them and what we are going to give in return. It is a document we don't need to refer to as much these days, but it is an important safety net.

As a parent of a pupil at Parklands Primary School, I/we will:

- Make sure my child arrives at school by 8.50am, properly dressed and equipped.

- Make sure my child attends every day and notify the school of reasons for any absence through ill-health.

- Not take my child out of school for family holidays during term time.

- Make arrangements for my child's safe return home at the appropriate time.

- Support my child's learning, ensuring the completion of homework set and their participation in any school trips and visits.

- Support the school's policies and guidelines for learning, attendance, equality, discipline and good behaviour.

- Let the school know about any concerns that might affect my child's work or behaviour.

- Read all the information sent home as this gives me important details of relevant policies, meetings, workshops, activities, newsletters and open days.

- Attend parents' evenings as well as other meetings about my child's progress.

This contract is balanced with clear expectations for the children and details about how the school will support both parents and children, including:

- Providing the highest standard of primary education, giving all children equal opportunities to fulfil their potential.

- Encouraging children to believe in themselves, to feel valued and to support their spiritual, moral, cultural and social development.

- Teaching children to develop a positive attitude to others, regardless of gender, race, culture, belief, values or age.

- Caring for children's safety and happiness in a supportive environment.

When Ofsted arrived in 2017, alarm bells were ringing for the inspector because 45 parents turned up to see them. With that number they were expecting only one thing – bad news. But, in fact, it was the complete reverse. For example, the parent who had previously declared, 'Over my dead body is my child going to Parklands,' explained how well her child had developed and that they loved being at the school so much that she had turned down a place at her preferred school six months later. The inspector had never in their career seen such positivity from parents.

Parklands Fundamentals

- What is the Christmas Eve moment for your school? What are you doing that goes over and above what is expected?

- Every child deserves to see Santa. Every child deserves a present. Every child deserves a special Christmas lunch in an atmosphere that is happy and calm and doesn't involve adults drinking alcohol. Every child deserves some family time that is about them and for them.

- Parental relationships are always proactive. The school makes the first, second and third moves. The goodwill always pays back double.

- Tackling food poverty directly addresses the achievement gap. Children learn better when they are well nourished.

- Media attention can generate donations that make the hassle more than worthwhile.

- You don't abandon people when they are in trouble. You don't walk away when it gets difficult. Relationships are always two-way.

Collaboration is in the DNA of Parklands Primary School. Their innovative partnership stems from resourceful leaders working collaboratively for the benefit of the school and the local community. So much of what this outstanding school does will endure for years to come.

TES Schools Awards 2017

Chapter 8

Taking Care
of Business

Chapter 8

Taking Care of Business

Anyone who has ever taught a class of 30–35 children would say it is obvious that small classes are better for children's learning. The easier it is for the teacher to get around and talk to everyone, the better the chance for individual attention. It seems to be those who are distanced from education who assume that other things – like money and spreadsheets – are more important than the children.

Independent schools sell themselves on small class sizes and high adult-to-pupil ratios. The children at Parklands – indeed, all children – deserve nothing less. We use income from a variety of sources to lift adult–pupil ratios and drive down class sizes. It is an important aspect of what enables Parklands to bridge the attainment gap year on year. We are blessed that we get a large amount of pupil premium money. But it is also the money that is donated by national and international companies which helps to ensure that we can remove every barrier to achievement. It pays for an unprecedented 36 teaching assistants across 15 classes. It allows us to do so much more.

Of course, the politicians always tell us that state schools should take their example from independent schools. I am happy to learn from any school (and we are partnered with some brilliant ones); just give us all the same budget so that we start from the same place.

Buildings and Maintenance

When I set the budget every April, we put £150,000–200,000 into buildings and maintenance. Like many schools built in the 1920s, wear and tear is a constant drain on the finances.

I spoke to Kevin McCabe, the managing director of Thorpe Park Leeds and GMI Construction Group near Wetherby. I said, 'Look, my class-rooms are in urgent need of redecoration. The paint is peeling off the walls. They look an absolute shambles. When you take on apprentices, instead of getting them painting on a white wall and then cleaning it off the next day, send them to my school and they can decorate the class-rooms. It'll brighten the place up and give them real work experience.' (I also mentioned that I was a Blades fan as Kevin is also the chairman of Sheffield United PLC.)

It seemed to land at the right time. Kevin said, 'We love this idea for our apprentices, but we would like to go one step further. We're going to shut down for two days and we're going to send the entire workforce into your school. We're going to decorate every single classroom for you.' People really want to help; you just need to make it easy for them to do so. Our classrooms have never looked better and everyone who participated had a brilliant time.

Another connection from Thorn Lighting got to hear of the classroom redecoration project. They got in touch and visited the school. 'Well, you can't leave all that shoddy lighting up. Look at the state of it,' they said. 'We'll renew all of your lighting throughout the school for free.' So, as well as the redecorating, we got £200,000 worth of new lighting. There is momentum in giving.

Around the same time, I saw that Leeds College of Building was running courses for young people who had dropped out of education. A lot of schools are wary of inviting youngsters with a history of exclusion into their schools. We welcomed them with open arms and, under the direc-tion of the college, they decorated the school hall and gymnasium. That saved us another £29,000.

Between them, these organisations blitzed the whole school over the summer holiday. They did absolutely everything. I came back from my holiday to do some interviews with BBC Radio 5 Live and *Look North*. During the *Look North* interview, I mentioned that the only thing we would have to pay for was the paint. Then Dulux got in touch and said they would give us all of the paint for free. (Although, when I was interviewed by Radio 5 Live, a slip of the tongue meant that people thought Durex had donated the paint!) People do beautiful things – sometimes without even being asked. They see that the ball is already rolling, so it is easy for them to join in.

We work very closely with Unilever, who sponsor our library and science club. A senior executive who runs their European division visited the UK. He wanted to see a school, so they brought him to Parklands. He had a lovely time, talking to the children and staff, and soaking up the experience. As he left, he pulled out his cheque book and wrote us a cheque for £3,000. I didn't ask him for money; we just offered friendship. He could see the need for himself.

I think that a lot of head teachers are afraid to ask for contributions from businesses because they see it as a sign of weakness or desperation. There is no shame in attracting more money that directly benefits the children. I cannot wait for government to plug the funding crisis. The children only get one chance.

It is so important to have time with business people face to face. It is about building that relationship, inviting them into your assemblies and doing something special for them. For example, when we staged the school show, *High School Musical*, we ended up doing seven performances because we wanted to invite all the employees from all the companies who had helped us out to watch it. We needed them to see what these kids can produce if you have shown them love and hold on to a dream.

Times Tables Rock Stars and the Best Seats in the House assembly are two of our biggest strengths. Even if business people come in on a Tuesday, say, we run snippets of that assembly so they can experience Parklands in full flow. We can turn it on in an instant.

It is always fun to see bankers, accountants and high-powered executives joining in a times table face-off with a 5- or 6-year-old. You can see them thinking, I'll let this 5-year-old win the first two or three rounds and then I'll start trying. Before they know it, the kids are thrashing them. They are utterly floored by their speed and accuracy. Sometimes they mention that their own children go to an expensive private school and don't even know their times tables!

We have brilliant partnerships with businesses like TD Direct Investing. They have assured me that they will employ the first child from Parklands who goes to university. We have got some of the brightest children here, who just need to have a chance to be believed in and shine. TDI know what we are about and believe in what we do because they have been here, tasted the Parklands experience and have made a real connection with the school.

Mike Harvey from Business in the Community was a big influence on me when I first started at Parklands. Mike was the person who helped me with business links from day one. In that initial year, he was pivotal in getting all the businesses involved. It was his expertise that guided us and his contacts that were so important. He got them through the door and then I sold the school to them, like a mixture of Del Boy and Arthur Daley! It worked immediately. People were inspired by our story and motivated to contribute. And they didn't just invest once. One generous donor visited us and as he was leaving, unprompted, wrote out a personal cheque to the school for £5,000. These are serious people who donate year on year. So, Mike Harvey, Business in the Community; great man, vital role.

The worst thing about Parklands when I arrived was the toilets. You know the sort: old-fashioned ones with a high-level porcelain cistern, metal chain and wooden pull that has been yanked by 10,000 children. If one of the cisterns fell it would probably go straight through the floor. Not toilets for the 21st century. I knew I needed to find £145,000 for new facilities.

Officially, Parklands is a one-and-a-half form entry school with space for 45 new children to join each year. When there is a bulge in the birth rate, the local authority are often keen to negotiate a higher number of places. Such negotiations can bring benefits to all the children. On the condition of Parklands taking higher numbers in 2021, we got a new state-of-the-art toilet block. Being successful now brings its own opportunities.

We have absorbed four bulges in the last seven years. As a result, we have been able to fund two new toilet blocks (£245,000), changed a toilet block into a classroom (£120,000), renovated our resource provision – increasing from seven places to 14 places to 21 places (£140,000) and replaced some windows (£250,000). We have also updated six classrooms, which means new whiteboards, tables, carpets, fixtures and fittings, as well as decoration. If you are brave enough and stick to your guns, there is always a deal to be done that works in the best interests of the children.

Safeguarding for Visitors

Schools must create safe environments for children and young people through robust safeguarding practices. With so many visitors coming into the school, our safeguarding practices need to be really good. Some visitors spend their days in very different working environments and with different values. A safeguarding meeting is always the first step. This gives us an opportunity to do much more than just an ID check.

We make it very clear to visitors what our expectations of their behaviour are. We leave nothing to chance. Simple things that educators do every day are not always obvious to people from outside schooling. For example, we always encourage our visitors to talk to the children, but never on a one-to-one basis in a room on their own. This is second nature to teachers, but for business people visiting for the day we need to be explicit about what is expected. Groups leaders must have a Disclosure and Barring Service check and everyone is checked against List 99.[1]

We want people to come and visit. We want them to have a great time. We want the children to meet lots of interesting, inspirational (and safe) adults. We want it to be a successful and brilliant day. Therefore, we are very careful to perform the necessary checks and to coach them well. We

---

1   List 99 is a confidential register of individuals who have been barred from working with children by the Department for Education.

introduce our visitors to the five different child protection officers in school – and make sure their photographs are all over the building too. We ensure that everyone knows who to go to if they have an issue that they need to discuss. My office door is always open. It is critical to make sure the staff are well trained in how to respond to concerns; with the right practice and good vigilance everyone can be safe. Even though our safeguarding is strong, we always want to learn more and do more. Everyone needs to feel safe in school, regardless of what event or visits are going on.

Safeguarding does not just impact on the children; it allows visitors more access and dramatically improves their experience of being in school. I often encourage business people to visit other schools I know, but sometimes the feedback can be difficult to hear. It is often the same: 'We can't go back there again. It was supposed to be a day away from the desk doing something interesting and worthwhile. But nobody spoke to us. We weren't allowed to go anywhere. It was like being in a prison for the day: you can't do this. You can't do that. No, you can't have your lunch there.' It can be really challenging for them.

Explain the rules promptly and clearly so these problems disappear. Robust safeguarding practices allow school visits to be a more enjoyable experience for everyone. The more informed you are, the sharper the boundaries and the better the experience. Simple.

Lockdown Laptops

During the second lockdown the school had no laptops for pupils. On the Friday before the October half-term break, the Department for Education sent an email saying how marvellous they were (not unusual) and that they had an additional 500,000 laptops to issue to schools. They requested that we checked their website to see our new allocation. I logged on excitedly hoping to find that our allocation of 67 had increased to the 200-plus I had calculated we would need. We had been allotted just three! I was fuming with the Department for Education, and not for the first time during the pandemic. They had cut our measly allocation of

67 to an almost useless three. It was scandalous. I wasn't happy and made a fuss. We ended up on the BBC, ITV and Sky News.

But the anger wasn't in vain. As a result of the media appearances, 250 people sent donations to the school, which meant we could buy laptops from London Grid for Learning (https://lgfl.net) at a heavily discounted price and from the brilliant guys at LetsLocalise (www.letslocalise.co.uk) who supplied nearly 200 laptops and tablets to the school. The charities have been great. People's compassion is huge. They were wondering, like us, how we could get children doing online learning if no one had a laptop.

Ben Chapman from ITV came to do a live interview about schools that were still waiting to receive their laptops. Ten minutes before we went live, Ben was talking to the then Secretary of State for Education Gavin Williamson's people in front of me, over the phone, and eight minutes later my secretary came into my office saying she had an email from the Department for Education stating that our laptops would arrive the following day. They had increased our allocation of three to 11 laptops; we got our full allocation of 67 four months later. I put out a tweet thanking the media for their support. The Department for Education insisted that this was just a coincidence. Yeah, right!

The media can be a powerful ally; they have certainly given Parklands and our families a voice. Schools are often wary of the media, but involve them at the right time, with the right story, and it doesn't just invite attention on to the work you are doing, it attracts resources too.

Tips to Get the Most Out of Media Opportunities

- Do your homework and make notes. Think about how your comments will be received by the profession.
- Don't accept last-minute requests when you are unsure of the topic. Be confident if an interviewer throws you a curveball. Go back to your notes and what you want to say. Make sure you get your top three points across regardless of the questions you are asked.

- Say what you want to say in the first few sentences. You might not get much time and they might cut you off.

- If you are prerecording an interview, don't be afraid to stop and ask to do that bit again.

- Don't try to memorise your script – it needs to feel natural. However, you need to be able to look at the camera, not at your notes.

- Always bring it back to the children and the benefit to the school.

- Build a relationship with journalists and producers. They will keep your number and pass it on.

- Share when the best times of the day are for you and your school. Some schools can be ready at 8am while others are at their best at midday.

- Be prepared to be dropped. Let the children know this is a possibility.

- Do local TV and radio to get some experience.

Funding

We draw money into Parklands from a range of sources, but the £350,000–400,000 we bring in every year to make up our shortfall isn't necessarily cash. From commercial businesses to social enterprises and third sector charities and organisations, we work with all of them in different ways. As you may well be able to tap into the same national providers or find your local equivalents, I thought it would be useful to outline some of these relationships.

Some routes to revenue are long-winded and consume a great deal of time. Often these are fruitless pursuits so it is best not to waste time on them. One application we never do any more, because I got bored of always getting rejected, is the National Lottery. It seems you don't get anything from the National Lottery unless you represent a cricket or a tennis club. The grants involve pages and pages of forms, and ours are always refused on a technicality.

One of the biggest and best things that came out of COVID-19 was finding a social enterprise company called LetsLocalise (www.letslocalise .co.uk). LetsLocalise host schools' wish-lists which they aim to fulfil using local business contacts. When we experienced the debacle over the laptops they saw us on TV and got in touch straight away. We gave them the links to the TV interviews, they put us on their platform and got us 250 laptops. Amazing! In fact, they got us so many laptops, donated from firms like Legal & General, that we have refitted the entire ICT suite. Legal & General are our biggest sponsors now. The company saw the national disgrace over laptops and the fact that the neediest kids didn't have them. They offered 100, and then suddenly there were lots of companies donating laptops. LetsLocalise centralised it all and distributed them according to need.

When we needed wireless dongles, LetsLocalise and their partners gave us so many dongles that we ended up having enough to give one to every child. They were absolutely key during the lockdowns as they were able to react much faster than government. LetsLocalise are now starting to source school uniforms and are centralising purchasing to get better deals.

The Henry Smith Charity (www.henrysmithcharity.org.uk) is one of the few organisations that funds school trips. A lot of the rules for accessing pots of money prevent schools from using it for school trips. The Henry Smith Charity understands that the most deprived kids don't get a holiday. You can apply for up to £2,500, which pays for two of the four residentials we organise. The five £2,500 grants we get fund the Whitby trip and the coach costs for the Year 3 science trip. It is a great charity, and there is a simple form to fill in.

The SHINE trust (https://shinetrust.org.uk) was based in Kings Cross, London, but because of the big government push on the Northern Powerhouse (now relabelled as 'levelling up'), they relocated to Leeds. The SHINE trust provides grants for schools in the North of England which want to undertake ambitious projects. It isn't exclusively for those from the most deprived areas; you can be a leafy lane school and still tap into the SHINE trust. We have had four successful bids. We are particularly proud of an innovative project that directly targets a reduction in exclusion when children move to high school.

Exclusion

We don't exclude at Parklands. We have had one permanent exclusion in seven years, but, of course, it is a different story when it comes to high school because that is when exclusions can really begin in earnest. We wanted to do something positive to reduce the number of exclusions. We have seen too many children make it all the way through Parklands with great support, and then they find themselves out of their depth within weeks at high school.

It is hard going moving from a year group of 45 children to one of 400 children. However well we prepare them for that transition, it is difficult to anticipate how rough it can be. We felt that employing a learning mentor to work with our Year 6 pupils, who would follow them into high school, would have a direct and positive impact – especially as 85–90% of the children leaving Parklands transfer to the same school. The learning mentor moves into Year 7 with the pupils and works with them from September through to Easter. This helps them to settle in and carry their personal discipline from Parklands into a new environment. The learning mentor then returns to Parklands at Easter to work with the new Year 6 cohort.

This cycle has had a positive effect on the exclusion rate at the local high school, which has dropped significantly over the last two years. The SHINE trust funds all of that. What a result! Such has been the impact of the project that I was invited to deliver the keynote speech at the first Northern Powerhouse event, along with Manchester United and England player Gary Neville. More accolades for Parklands!

The best thing about the SHINE trust is that they want you to succeed. When you submit your application, a member of the panel will contact you and offer feedback: 'Right, we just need you to say how you are going to do this …'. There is a drafting process and they support you throughout. It is a team approach. Where it is difficult to get a grant from the National Lottery, the SHINE trust is much simpler and comes with lots of assistance. The SHINE trust don't donate cash, but they will fund a member of staff or resources for specific projects.

There are voluntary, non-profit action groups all over the country. We have had groups come in and build a sensory garden with gorgeous wooden archways. If you are in an old, battered school like ours, then making the grounds look attractive is vital. These kids don't have a lot at home, but they walk into paradise when they see the transformation that has taken place at school. It is worth searching for local voluntary action groups for small, manageable projects that don't require tradespeople.

Tips to Improve Your Revenue Streams

- Talk to people who are in business. Who do you know? What contacts do the staff/governors/trustees have? Who has a network you can tap into? Search on Google Maps and find out what national and multinational companies are based near you. If you are in Belfast, Leeds, Manchester, Glasgow or London, you can go to the top because most big businesses have a headquarters in one of these major cities. Wherever you are, though, there will be companies you haven't heard of on your doorstep willing to help and just waiting to be asked to start a relationship with your school.

- Build relationships, don't just ask for money. What opportunities can you offer that a company might find valuable? How can you enable them to fall in love with your vision, your dream and your school?

In larger companies, find out who the community champion is and invite them to showcase your school. Have a plan ready. When they ask what you need, be specific. Know what you want in each instance. Asking for a donation to the school fund is not going to encourage anyone, but a bench with their company name on it or a chicken coup with hens named after key employees might just seal the deal!

Check out Business in the Community (www.bitc.org.uk) which aims to bring companies and communities together. The Prince of Wales is the founding patron. Many businesses and public sector companies offer employees special leave for corporate volunteer days or volunteering time off. If you need to decorate your corridors, you may have a team of 60 people who can come in and spruce up your entire school in a single day. Make that the best day ever and you will have sown 60 seeds that will grow into more corporate contributions.

Three years ago, we hosted something called a Giving Game Day, which involved inviting 180 business people into school on the same day. We set up challenges based around a range of activities. Yes, some people were painting the fences, but they were interspersing it with penalty shootouts, times table challenges and even water fights! They are away from their desk for a day, and they feel they are really contributing to society as opposed to looking at a screen. They want to give something back, but we have to treat them in the same way that we treat a member of our own staff.

Companies give discounts on everything, yet many schools simply pay the label price without even asking for a reduction. There are deals to be made when you are spending hundreds or thousands of pounds. A 10% discount is easy and is often offered immediately when you ask. But work the story – highlight the benefits of being associated with your school, be cheeky – and you will not only get a 15% or 20% discount, but you might find they want to throw in some freebies too.

- Consider using your facilities for barter rather than renting out for cash. The opportunities for enriching the curriculum are huge. You can trade spaces for resources, and you will save time by not dealing with money out and money in. It is a much better trade.

- Every local house builder by law must give a percentage of their profits to local community projects. Find your local developers and start talking to them and inviting them in.

The feedback the school gets, and the reputation it now has, is well known all over Seacroft and all over Leeds. In fact, you could even argue all over the country: anyone on social media is likely to have heard of Parklands. People know about us because our message is always full of love. The community really relishes this. When the kids come home saying, 'We've just been filmed singing "Sweet Caroline" for the Euro Finals!' and are then on the telly, parents in the community just can't do enough to support the school and its ethos.

Parklands Fundamentals

- Never be afraid to ask for contributions on behalf of your children. And never be deterred if they say no. There are plenty more fish in the sea.

- Build face-to-face relationships. Bring people into school. Make them feel like they belong. Value their time.

- Be strong in your training and expectations of visitors around safeguarding. Make sure they know how to behave around the children. They may work in a completely different culture where different behaviours are acceptable. Don't take any chances.

- Use the levers that are already there – contributions from developers, community champions and people tasked with social responsibility agendas.

- You already know what you want from businesses. Try to focus on what experiences and enhancements you can provide for them as a first step. It is not all about cash; it is about time and services too.

- Sometimes head teachers need to speak out. Sometimes it gets results.

- Make the media work for you and your pupils.

When I first met Chris it was love at first sight! The passion for his school and his children shone from him and I was smitten! I had grown up only three miles from Seacroft and can still feel the fear that flowed through us as children when anyone uttered the word 'Seacroft'. Who would have thought that now, almost four years later, I would be on the governing body of Parklands Primary School, writing mentor to the school and still as much in love and awe of the most charismatic man I have ever met in my life.

Ros Wilson, author, education consultant
and governor of Parklands School

Conclusion

In my heart of hearts, do I really believe we are an outstanding school? I don't think there is such a thing as outstanding because you can always get better. We know that we aren't even halfway to achieving Parklands' full potential. It is nice to be recognised, but it is vitally important that we don't sit back and sing our own praises: 'Look at us, look at what we can do!'

As well as driving forward with new initiatives, we want to support other schools too. We give all of our policy documents away for free at www.parklandsprimary.org.uk, so that schools can take what they need from them. We want to be able to help other schools in the same way that other people have helped us, so we invite in leaders to look around and share our experience. We don't keep our work secret because we know that more schools can lead with love. We want to give them the confidence to do so. Our duty is to share what we know, to spread Parkland's love and to show everyone there is another way. A more inclusive and more successful way.

I will leave you with this anecdote as I think it sums up beautifully the impact of the Parklands experience on even the most stern-faced. At the end of a long day during the last school inspection, the lead inspector looked me in the eye, took a deep breath and said, 'You are an outstanding school.' A little tear meandered its way down my cheek and dropped onto the desk. A lovely happy tear. I looked up and three of the four inspectors had tears in their eyes too. I managed to hug them all before they left. Nobody leaves Parklands without a hug, not even an inspector! We are a school built on love, after all.

It is a fact that it is your school which is the inspiration. I have never left a school with such a buzz and sense of real achievement. Every member of staff, every child lifted me and I am sure that the other judges felt similarly proud to have been part of it. I have had a great day. I have been at Parklands Primary School in Leeds and have been inspired by a wonderful staff and incredible children today. I have to say that it is a credit to the city of Leeds. They are a wonderful school and made me feel so welcome as well.

Harry Gration, BBC Look North

Postscript: Jason

The sad death of our IT technician, Jason Kelk, in June 2021 sent shock-waves through all of us. Words are never enough. We hold him close to our hearts.

When I took over at Parklands we had a funding crisis, so I had to reorganise the staffing. This is always a difficult moment, and during the process many non-teaching staff were worried about their jobs. People react to this type of pressure in different ways. Jason came to see me and said, 'Just to let you know, boss, I'm going to leave and save you some money.' He was ready to throw in his job to help the school. It wasn't a joke; he was absolutely serious. That speaks to the kind of man he was.

I said, 'Jason, there are only two people safe from reorganisation in this school, and that's me and you. I'm safe because I'm doing the staff reduction process, so I can't be part of it, and you're safe too.' He said, 'Well, that's really kind. Why am I safe?' I said, 'Because I haven't got a clue what you do, so I haven't got a clue how to replace what you're doing!' We laughed – he loved that. We had a great relationship. He was a selfless man with true integrity.

Jason caught COVID-19 and was in hospital for a long time. In fact, he was the UK's longest hospitalised COVID-19 patient. I visited him during his illness. We made sure he knew that everyone at Parklands was thinking of him and missed him.

A few days before Jason died he was moved into St Gemma's Hospice. He asked to see me on what turned out to be his final day. He wanted to say goodbye to 'the boss'. His last wish outside his family was to say goodbye to me. I went immediately.

Jason was in a room with a tree outside the window. The leaves were fluttering and the sun was shining. It was a beautiful environment. Peaceful and calm. I spoke to him, tried to bring some love to him and his family, and then he closed his eyes for the last time. We all kissed his hand and said goodbye. He was brave and inspiring. He leaves behind a wife, step-children and grandchildren. We won't forget him. His family will always be close friends of mine and of Parklands. It hit everyone really hard.

He died on the Thursday, and there were lots of arrangements to be made. His wife, Sue, said to me, 'I don't know how I'm going to get all his belongings back from the hospital.' I gladly offered to retrieve his posses-sions. I said, 'I've got a school minibus. We'll come down and fetch his stuff.'

I had never before suffered a bereavement of someone so young; of a close colleague and friend. The only people I had known who had died were my grandparents, and it is built into us that we will lose our grand-parents at some point. Consequently, I was at sixes and sevens and not my normal self. The lovely Chris Bingham, our Year 3 teaching assistant, said, 'I'll come with you. Let's drive the minibus down to the hospital and get his things.'

When we arrived, I realised we would have difficulty pulling up where I had parked the week before. There were no spaces in the car park near the entrance. Even though we had a trolley, the nearest parking was a 15-minute walk from the hospital, and we needed to carry all his belongings.

In desperation, we snuck into the disabled bay. I thought, I might as well be honest, so I went and talked to the security guards. I said, 'Look, we're just emptying someone's room. We're in the disabled bay – it might take a couple of journeys.' The lovely people on security were brilliant. They just zoomed their camera around and said, 'Right, we've logged the reg-istration number. You're free for an hour.'

We went up to the intensive care unit on the fourth floor. They laughed when we walked in pulling our little trolley. They said, 'I don't think you realise how much stuff he's got.' The nurses brought out a big cage trolley like the ones they use in supermarkets for restacking the shelves. It was jam-packed with Jason's things. Then they brought out an itemised list, which covered 48 pages, and asked if we could go through and check everything off. I stopped them, thinking of the time limit on the parking and the sheer number of items. 'Listen, we're happy to work on trust here,' I said. 'We can't empty all that and put it in our little trolley. We might as well just take this big trolley and do it all in one go.' They weren't having it though: 'Oh, no, you can't do that. Health and safety. You need to have passed the trolley-pushing exam. There's nothing we can do – you've got to be a qualified porter to push the trolley.'

After we had said our goodbyes – they needed to get back to work – I said, 'Right, we'll start unloading. We'll have to make about 40 trips.' As the hospital staff disappeared around the corner, I looked at Chris, he looked at me and we both looked at the door. It was like *Thelma and Louise*. We grabbed the huge trolley we were unqualified to push and ran. We manoeuvred ourselves through the doors, sprinted round the corner, headed down in the lift and were off. Once in the main hospital we could cut through from one wing to another. There were restricted access corridors and people were opening up doors asking, 'Where are you going?' The power of a lanyard that says 'Staff' is amazing though. I just happened to be wearing my school lanyard. I rarely take it off. (Yes, I have slept in it before.) Dyson and lanyard are inseparable. People thought we were hospital staff, so every door was open for us on our mad and slightly naughty trolley dash.

We burst out of the hospital into the light, transferred all of Jason's possessions as quickly as we could and returned the trolley, all within the time limit the security officer had given us to park. As we started the van, rather out of breath, I said, 'Jason must be laughing his socks off watching us do this!' A little bit of anarchy. A little bit of rock 'n' roll. He would have loved it.

We are going to rename the ICT suite, put up a big plaque and call it the Jason Kelk ICT Suite. He was absolutely mad about a TV programme called *The IT Crowd*. I used to wonder what he was on about. Every time you rang him up, he would say, 'Have you tried turning it off and on again?' It took about three years before he explained to me that he was repeating a line from the show; so, we will also commemorate his favourite quote. And we will invite his family in to show them the impact he made – and continues to make – to our school.

Rest in peace, Jason. You will always be a part of Parklands.

About the Author

Chris Dyson is the proud head teacher of Parklands Primary School in Seacroft in Leeds. Chris was brought up in a single-parent household and received free school clothes and free school meals himself as a child, which has meant that the connection between his early life and that of Parklands' pupils is rooted in common experience.

Chris believes that education is the key to making the future brighter, and he is fuelled by a desire to provide his pupils with the best education and opportunities possible.

Independent Thinking on Restorative Practice

Building relationships, improving behaviour and creating stronger communities

Mark Finnis

ISBN 978-178135338-7

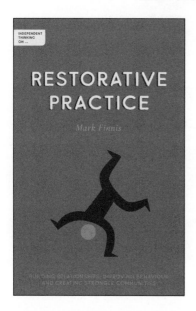

Drawing on his many years' experience working with schools, social services and local governments across the country, Mark shares all you need to know about what restorative practice is, how it works, where to start and the many benefits of embedding a relational approach into any educational organisation that genuinely has people at its heart.

Covering coaching circles and the power of doing things with (and not to) children and young people, to moving your values off lanyards and posters and into the lived experience of every member of the school community, this book sets out how restorative practice – when done well – can transform every aspect of school life.

The book shares advice on how to put behaviour right when it goes wrong in a more positive, less punitive way, and, more importantly, on how to get it right and keep it right in the first place. Furthermore, it advocates an approach that is collaborative, empowering and positive – and ultimately geared to improve motivation, engagement and independent learning in even the hardest-to-reach young people.

Suitable for school leaders, educators and anyone working with young people.

The Kindness Principle

Making relational behaviour management work in schools

Dave Whitaker

ISBN 978-1781353851-7

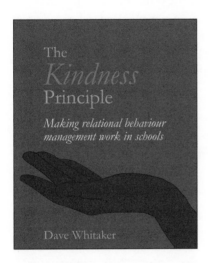

The Kindness Principle begins with the idea that relationships should be at the heart of behaviour management and culture, and sets out the ways in which the adoption of relational approaches can help create safer and happier schools. Schools where all staff and learners are valued and understood, where expectations and standards are high, and where kindness and acceptance matter.

Dave Whitaker explores why it is so important to understand children – offering techniques and advice on how to work effectively with all children (even the most challenging and troubled ones) without resorting to zero-tolerance, no-excuses and consequence-driven practices.

Dave also shares a wealth of real-life experiences from some of the most challenging schools in the country, along with research-informed insights that will help teachers understand children's behaviour in a new light. To this end he provides a wealth of guidance to help develop effective practice and learn from people who have actually walked the walk and don't just talk the talk.

Furthermore, the topics covered in the book include: restorative approaches, unconditional positive regard, building personal resilience, structures and routines, and the ins and outs of rewards and sanctions.

Suitable for teachers, school leaders and anyone working with children.

When the Adults Change, Everything Changes
Seismic shifts in school behaviour
Paul Dix

ISBN 978-178135273-1

Paul Dix upends the debate on behaviour management in schools and offers effective tips and strategies that serve to end the search for change in children and turn the focus back on the adults.

Suitable for all head teachers, school leaders, teachers, NQTs and classroom assistants – in any phase or context, including SEND and alternative provision settings – who are looking to upgrade their own classroom management or school behaviour plan.

After the Adults Change
Achievable behaviour nirvana
Paul Dix

ISBN 978-178135377-6

In this follow-up to his bestselling book *When the Adults Change, Everything Changes*, Paul Dix explains how teachers and school leaders can move beyond the behaviour management revolution and build a school culture rooted in relational practice.

Paul delves into the possibilities for improvement in pupil behaviour and teacher–pupil relationships, drawing further upon a hugely influential behaviour management approach whereby expectations and boundaries are exemplified by calm, consistent and regulated adults.